DOUBLE BASS BOOK 1

ESSENTIAL ELEMENTS for Strings

COMPREHENSIVE STRING METHOD

MICHAEL ALLEN • ROBERT GILLESPIE • PAMELA TELLEJOHN HAYES

ARRANGEMENTS BY JOHN HIGGINS

CONGRATULATIONS! You have made one of the most rewarding decisions in your life by joining the orchestra. The key to succeeding with *Essential Elements for Strings* is your commitment to daily practice. Each time you learn a new note, count a new rhythm, or play a melody with a friend, you become a more accomplished musician. As you continue to develop your skills, you will become increasingly aware of an abundance of opportunities that are available in the future. Musicians can teach, perform, conduct, or compose. No matter what profession you choose there are always opportunities available to you. You can play in community, civic, or church orchestras, attend concerts, and become a supporter of the arts. Whether you choose music as a vocation or avocation, we hope it will become an important part of your life. We are thrilled to welcome you to our orchestra family and wish you the very best for a lifetime of musical success.

HISTORY OF THE DOUBLE BASS

The string family includes the violin, viola, violoncello, and the double bass. The double bass (also called the 'string bass', or the 'bass' for short) is the most versatile of all the string instruments. At home in the symphony orchestra, jazz combo, concert band, and the dance band, the double bass provides the harmonic foundation in many styles of music.

The double bass sounds much lower than the cello and is tuned differently than the other instruments of the string family. Gasparo da Salo is credited with being the first to make a double bass in its present form. Other famous double bass makers include Carlo Guiseppe Testore, Carlo Bergonzi, and John Frederich Lott.

Nearly every composer has written music for the double bass, including Johann Sebastian Bach, Ludwig van Beethoven, and Peter Ilyich Tchaikovsky. Famous double bass performers include Gary Karr, Francois Rabbath, Ron Carter, Milt Hinton, Ray Brown, Edgar Meyer, Esperanza Spalding, and Hal Robinson.

To create an account, visit:
www.essentialelementsinteractive.com
Student Activation Code
E1DB-3522-7391-9919

ISBN 979-835012077-6

THE DOUBLE BASS

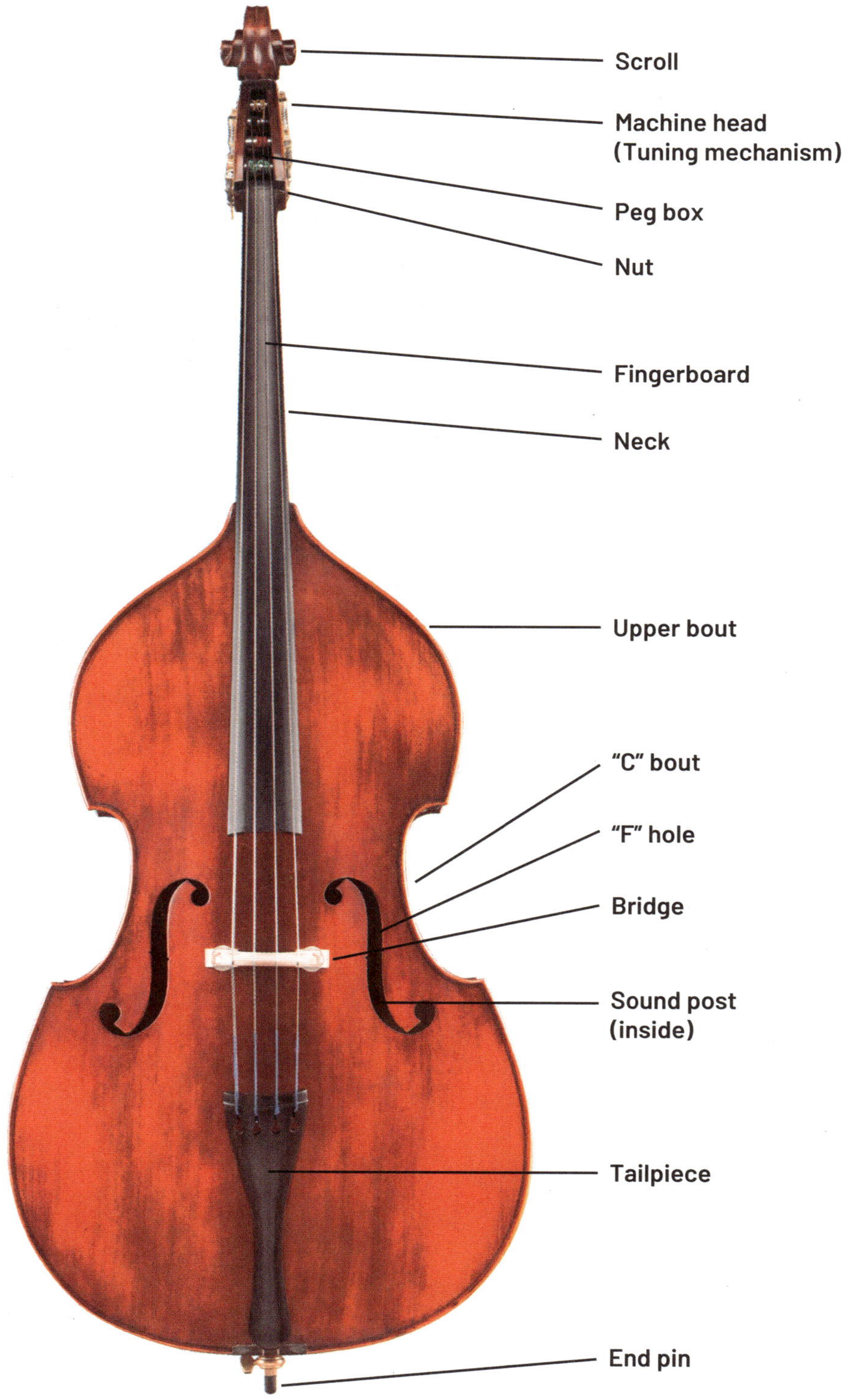
Scroll
Machine head
(Tuning mechanism)
Peg box
Nut
Fingerboard
Neck
Upper bout
"C" bout
"F" hole
Bridge
Sound post
(inside)
Tailpiece
End pin

Take Special Care

String instruments are delicate. Follow your teacher's guidelines in caring for your instrument, and it will last forever.

- Follow your teacher's instructions when removing the instrument from the case.
- Protect your instrument from heat, cold, and quick changes in temperature.
- Always wipe off the instrument with a soft dry cloth. Be sure to remove all fingerprints and rosin.

Accessories

- Rosin
- Soft cloth
- Stool (optional)

Instruments and photos courtesy of Eastman Music Company.

THE BOW

French
Tip
Stick
Bow hair
Winding
Ferrule
Frog
Adjusting
screw
German

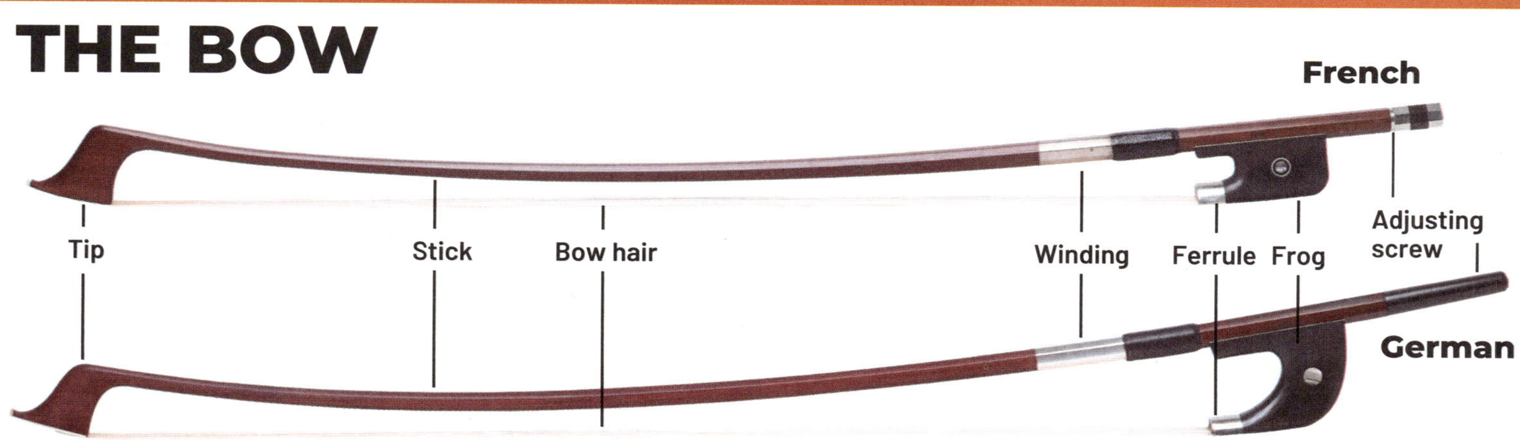

- Never touch the bow hair.

Holding Your Instrument

The best way to learn to play your instrument is to practice one skill at a time. Repeat each step until you are comfortable demonstrating it for your teacher and classmates.

Holding The Double Bass (sitting)

Step 1 Remove the bow from the case and put it in a safe place. Open the case and remove the bass. Identify all parts of the bass.

Step 2 Adjust the length of the end pin so that the nut of the bass is near the top of your forehead when standing.

Step 3 Sit squarely on the front half of the stool with your right foot on the floor and your left foot on a rung of the stool. Place the end pin in front of your left foot about one arm's length away.

Step 4 Rotate the bass slightly to the right and lean the bass toward your body so that the upper bout rests against the left side of your stomach. Identify the letter names of each string: E (lowest pitch), A, D, G. Raise your right index finger over the strings and pluck them as directed by your teacher. Plucking the strings is called *pizzicato*, and is abbreviated *pizz*.

Holding The Double Bass (standing)

Step 1 Remove the bow from the case and put it in a safe place. Open the case and remove the bass. Identify all parts of the bass.

Step 2 Adjust the length of the end pin so that the nut of the bass is near the top of your forehead when standing.

Step 3 Place the end pin in front of your left foot about one arm's length away. Place your left foot slightly forward.

Step 4 Rotate the bass slightly to the right and lean the bass toward your body so that the upper bout rests against the left side of your stomach. Identify the letter names of each string: E (lowest pitch), A, D, G. Raise your right index finger over the strings and pluck them as directed by your teacher. Plucking the strings is called *pizzicato*, and is abbreviated *pizz*.

The student shown is a member of the Milwaukee Youth Symphony Orchestra.

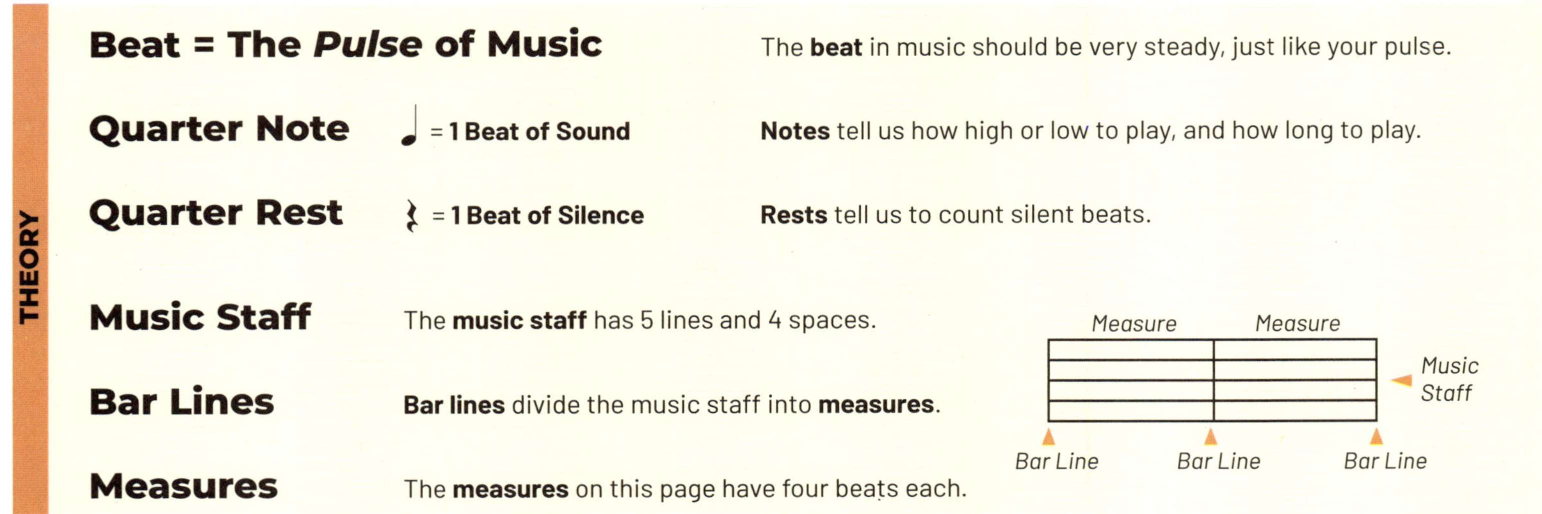

1. TUNING TRACK

Wait quietly for your teacher to tune your instrument.

2. LET'S PLAY "OPEN D"

Pizzicato (pizz.) ◄ *Pluck the strings*

0 ◄ *Open string*

D

D D D | D D D | D D D D | D D D

3. LET'S PLAY "OPEN A"

A

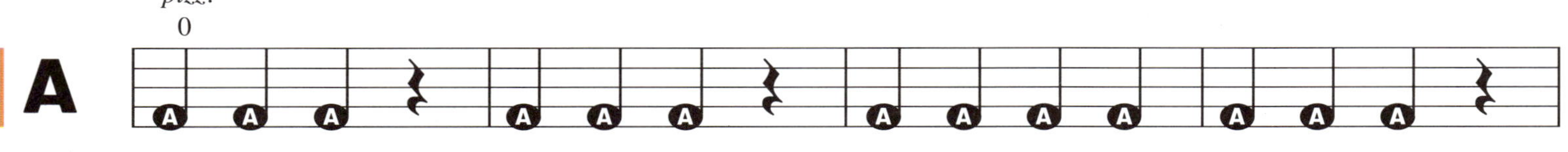

Keep a steady beat.

4. TWO'S A TEAM

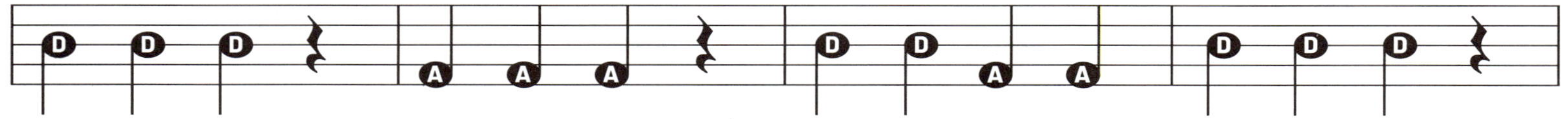

5. AT PIERROT'S DOOR

The melody is included on the online audio.

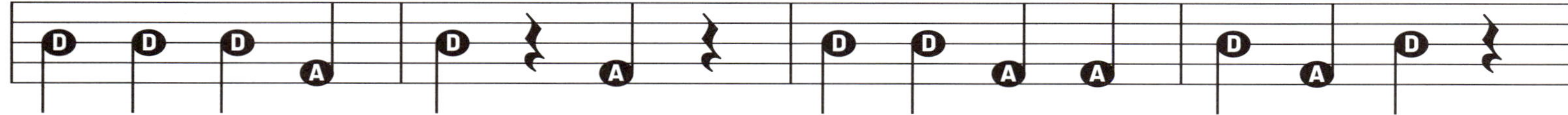

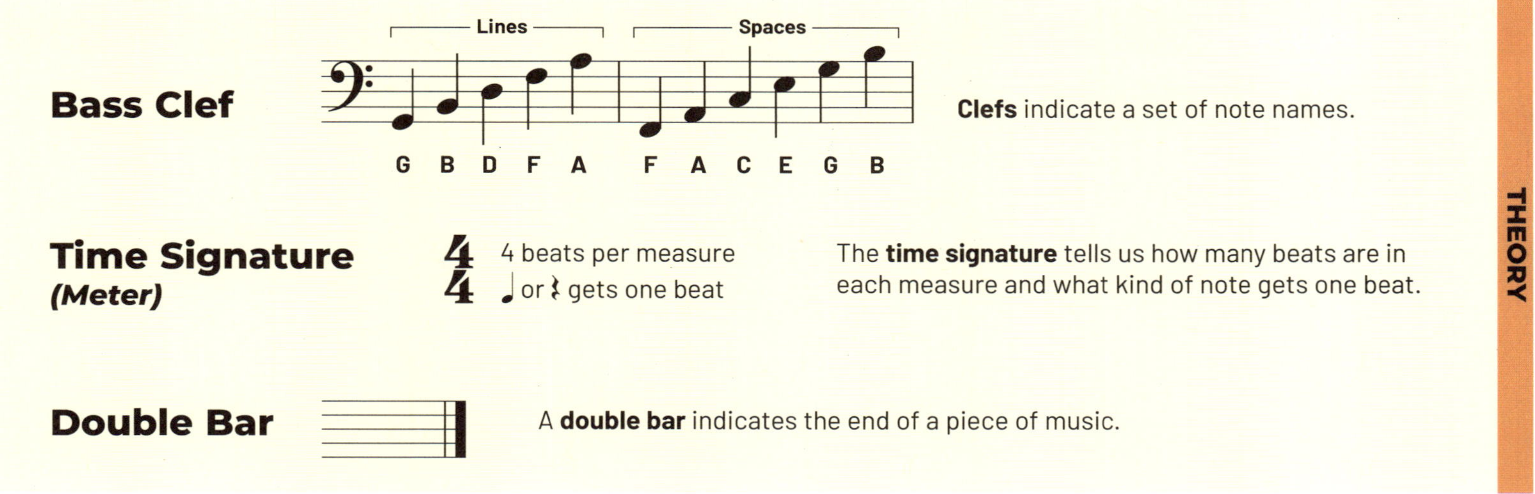

Bass Clef — **Clefs** indicate a set of note names.

Time Signature ***(Meter)*** — 4/4: 4 beats per measure; ♩ or 𝄽 gets one beat. The **time signature** tells us how many beats are in each measure and what kind of note gets one beat.

Double Bar — A **double bar** indicates the end of a piece of music.

6. JUMPING JACKS *Identify the clef and time signature before playing.*

7. MIX 'EM UP

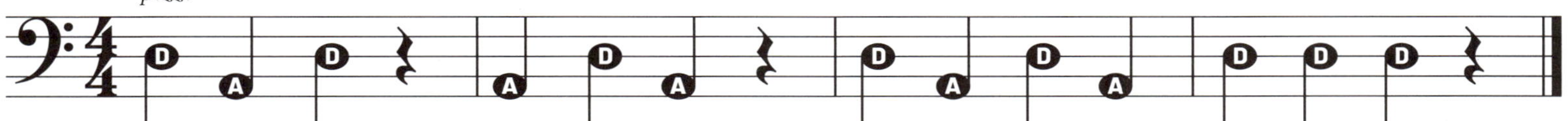

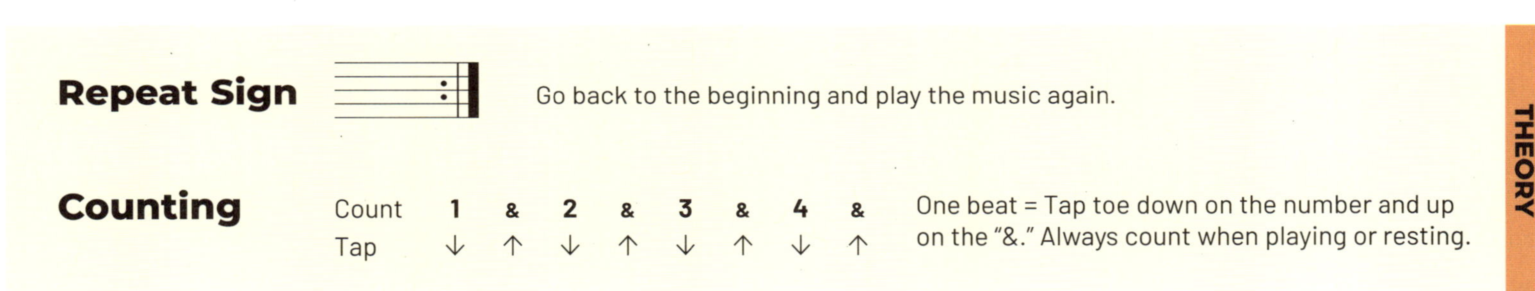

Repeat Sign — Go back to the beginning and play the music again.

Counting

Count	1	&	2	&	3	&	4	&
Tap	↓	↑	↓	↑	↓	↑	↓	↑

One beat = Tap toe down on the number and up on the "&." Always count when playing or resting.

8. COUNT CAREFULLY *Keep a steady beat when playing or resting.*

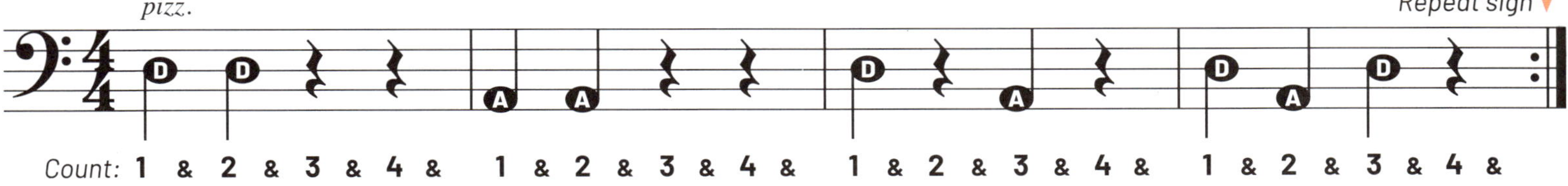

9. ESSENTIAL ELEMENTS QUIZ *Write in the counting before you play.*

SHAPING THE LEFT HAND

D STRING NOTES

Step 1 Shape your left hand as shown. Be certain your palm faces you.

0 = Open string
1 = 1st finger
2 = 2nd finger
3 = 3rd finger
4 = 4th finger

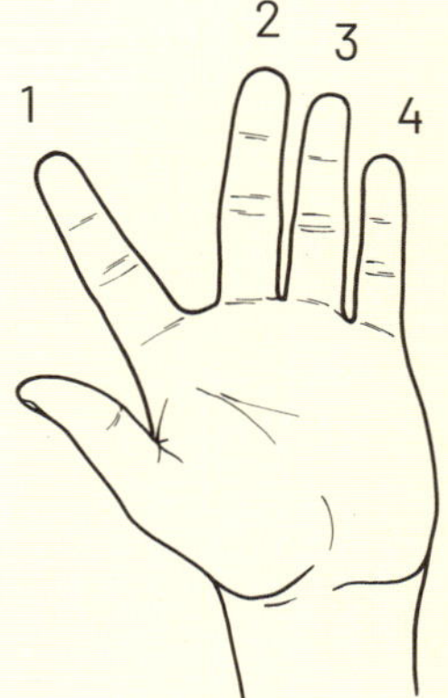

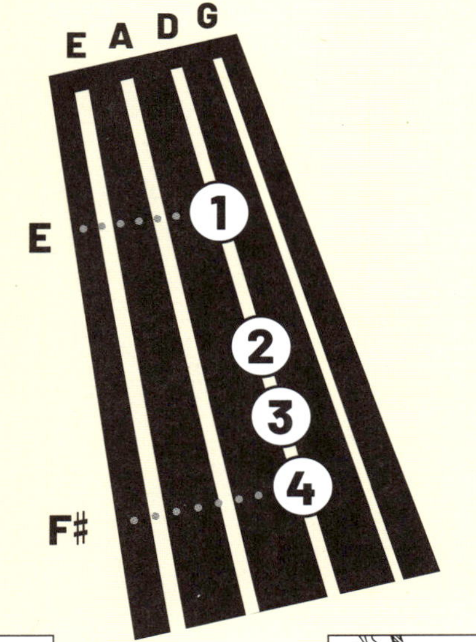

Step 2 Bring your left hand to the fingerboard. Place your fingers on the D string, keeping your hand shaped as shown. Be sure your thumb is behind the second finger and slightly bent.

F♯ is played with 4 fingers on the D string.

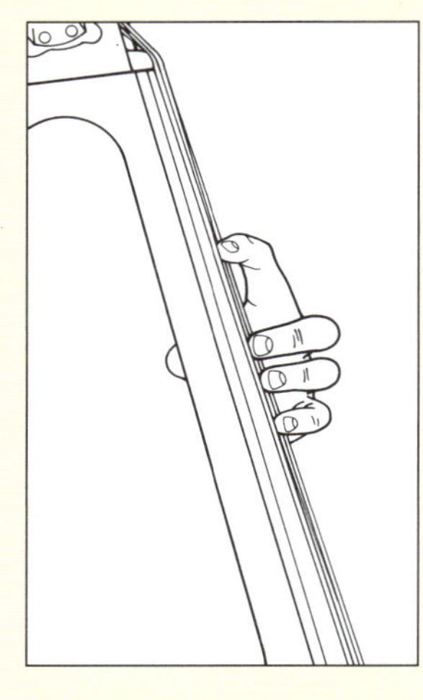

E is played with 1 finger on the D string.

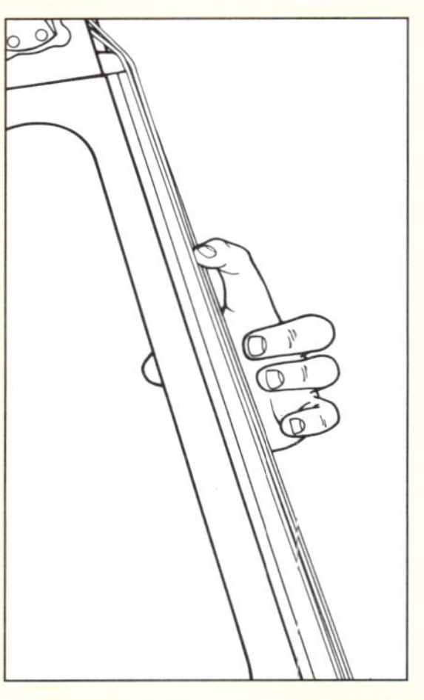

Listening Skills Play what your teacher plays. Listen carefully.

10. LET'S READ "G" *Start memorizing the note names.*

G

THEORY

Sharp ♯ A **sharp** sign raises the sound of notes and remains in effect for the entire measure. Notes without sharps are called **natural** notes.

11. LET'S READ "F♯" (F-sharp)

F♯

▲ *Play all F♯'s. Sharps apply to the entire measure.*

12. LIFT OFF

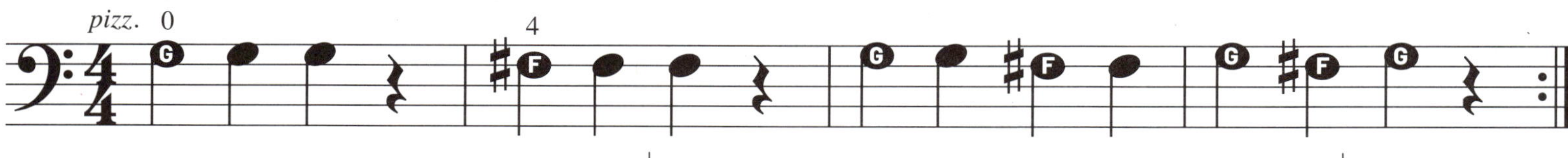

▲ *Keep fingers down when you see this bracket.*

 Is your left hand shaped as shown in the diagrams above?

 *See inside front cover for information on accessing instructional videos.*

SHAPING THE RIGHT HAND

BOW BUILDER ONE *(French)*

Bow Builder One is demonstrated on the online video, showing both French and German bow holds.

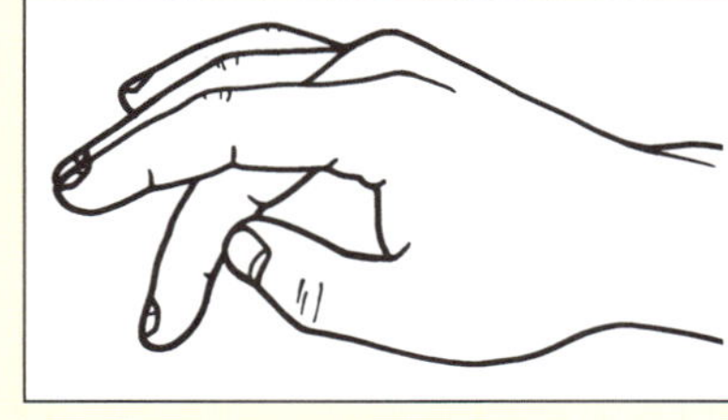

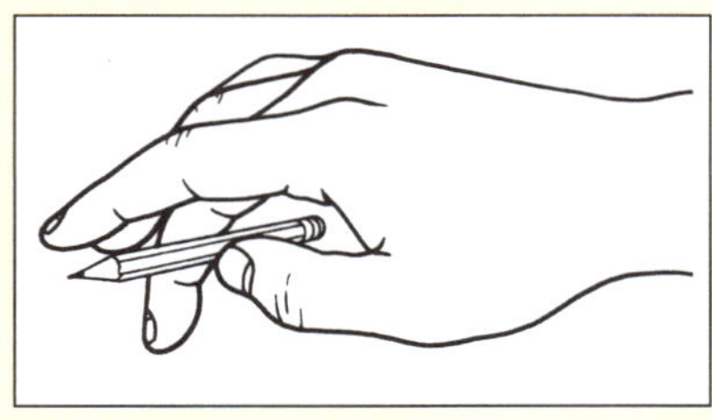

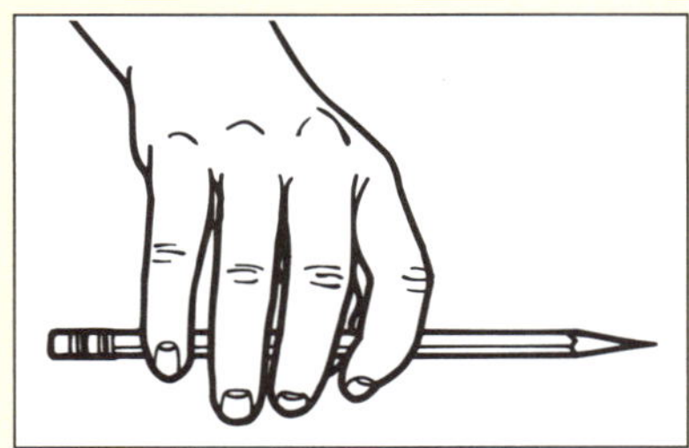

Pencil Hold

Step 1 Hold a pencil in your left hand about waist level.

Step 2 Place the tip of your right thumb between the first and second joints of your second finger.

Step 3 Place the pencil between your thumb and second finger, while keeping your thumb gently curved.

Step 4 The pencil should touch your first three fingers between the first and second joints, and touch the fourth finger at the first joint, as shown.

Step 5 Remove your left hand from the pencil. Keep your fingers relaxed. Practice shaping your hand on the pencil until it feels natural to you.

★ Practice BOW BUILDER ONE daily.

13. ON THE TRAIL *Say or sing the note names before you play.*

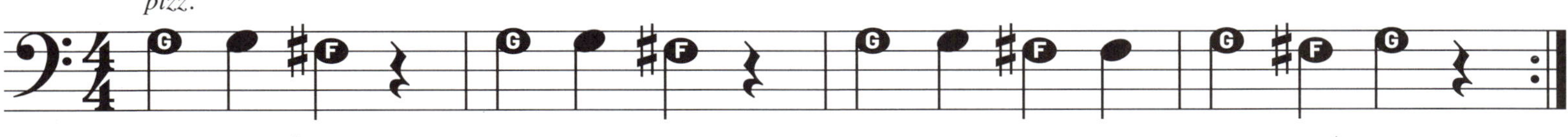

14. LET'S READ "E"

E

15. WALKING SONG

16. ESSENTIAL ELEMENTS QUIZ *Draw the missing symbols where they belong before you play:*

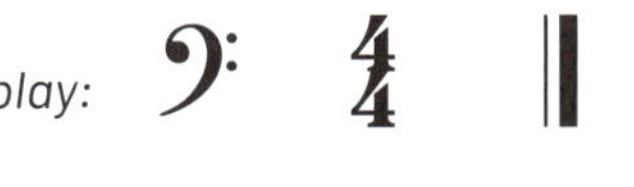

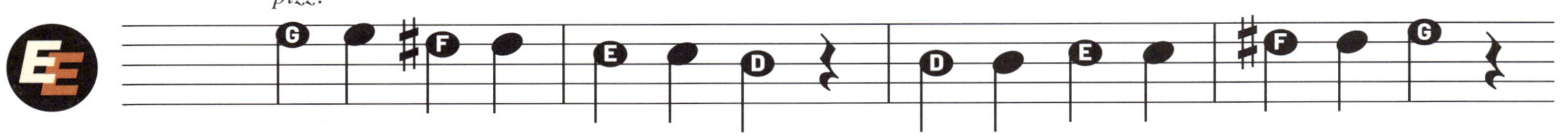

BOW BUILDER TWO

Pencil Hold Exercises *(French Bow Only)*

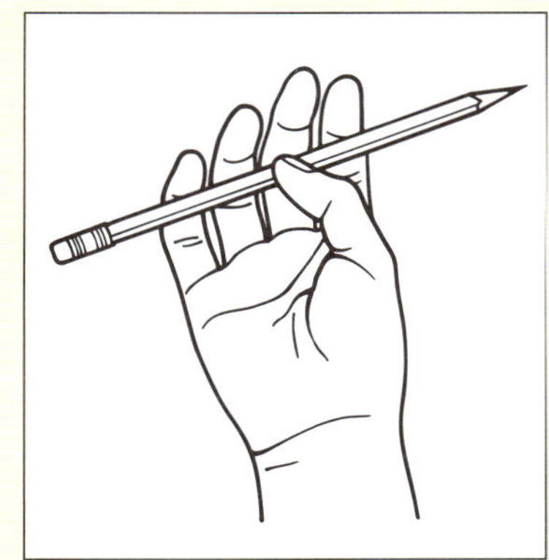
Knuckle Turnovers

I'm Outta Here
Wave good-bye while keeping your wrist relaxed.

Thumb Flexers
Flex your thumb in and out.

Finger Taps
Tap your first finger. Then tap your fourth finger.

Knuckle Turnovers
Turn your hand over and be sure your thumb knuckle is bent, as shown.

BOW BUILDER THREE

Bowing Motions

The Pendulum *(French and German Bow)*
Let your arm hand down to your side. While keeping your elbow straight, swing your arm back and forth like a pendulum.

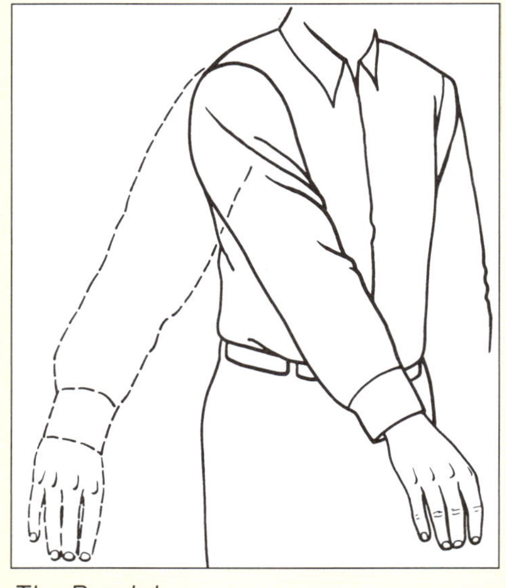
The Pendulum

17. HOP SCOTCH

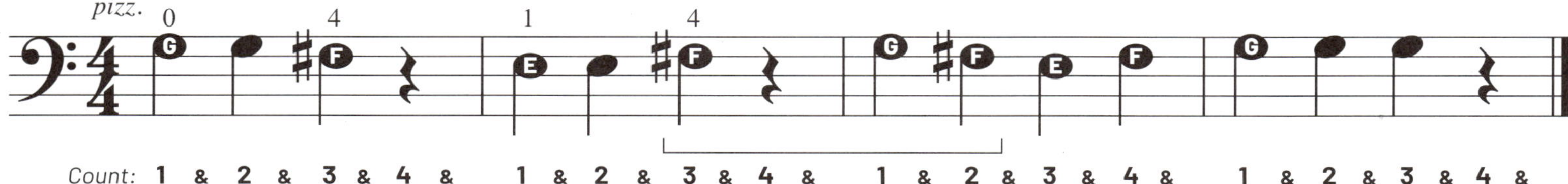

HISTORY

Folk songs have been an important part of cultures for centuries and have been passed on from generation to generation. Folk song melodies help define the sound of a culture or region. This folk song comes from the Slavic region of eastern Europe.

18. MORNING DANCE

Slavic Folk Song

19. ROLLING ALONG

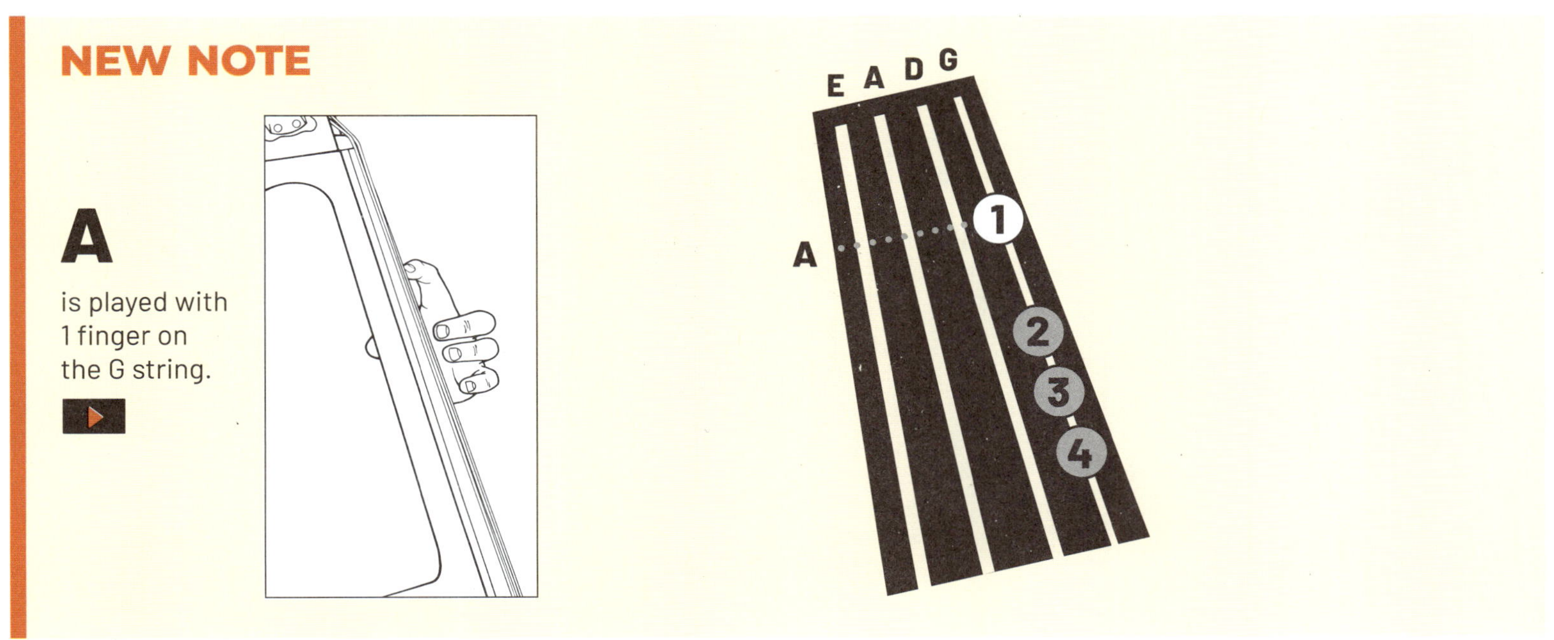

20. GOOD KING WENCESLAS

Welsh Folk Song

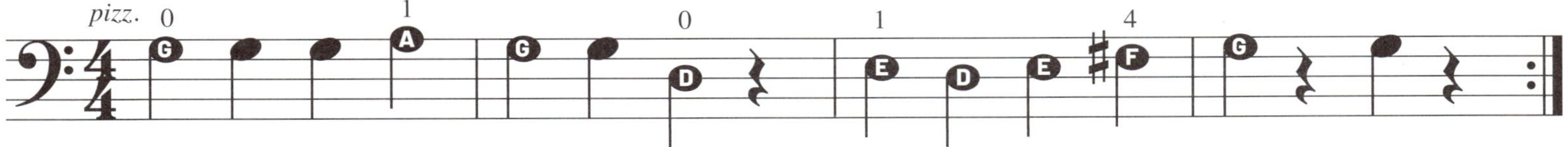

21. SEMINOLE CHANT

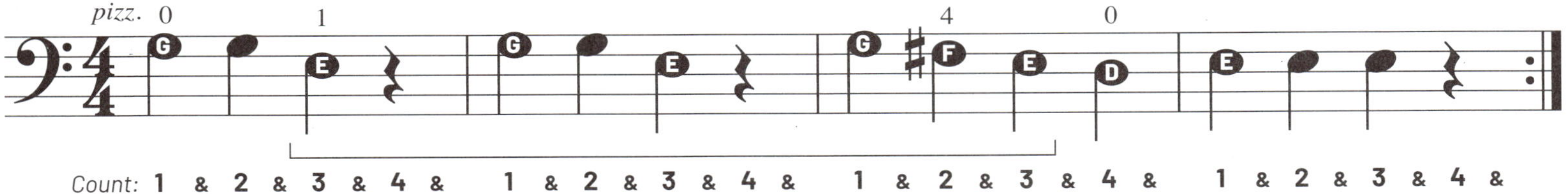

22. ESSENTIAL ELEMENTS QUIZ – LIGHTLY ROW

The left hand workouts "Finger Taps" and "Strummin' Along" are demonstrated on the online video.

G STRING NOTES

D is played with 4 fingers on the G string in third position (III).

C♯ is played with 2 fingers on the G string in third position (III).

B is played with 4 fingers on the G string in first position (I).

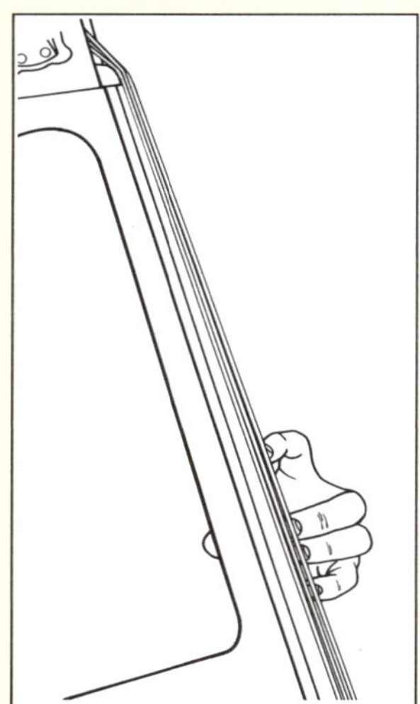

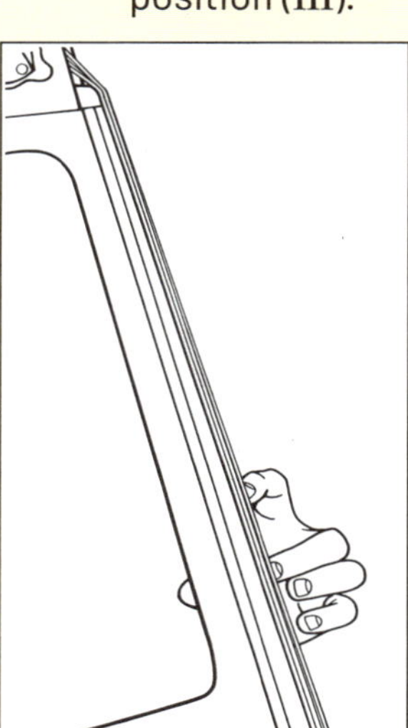

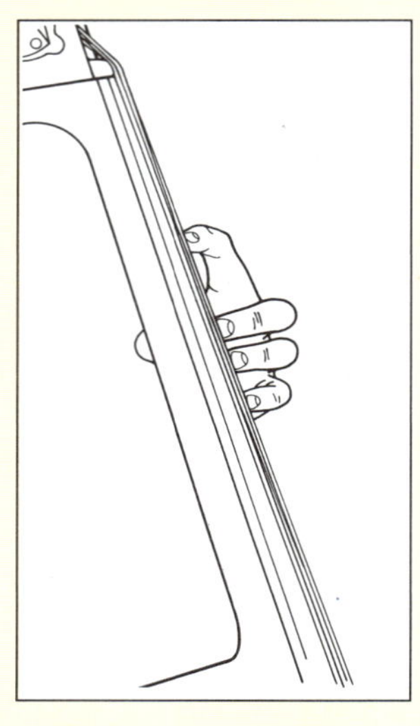

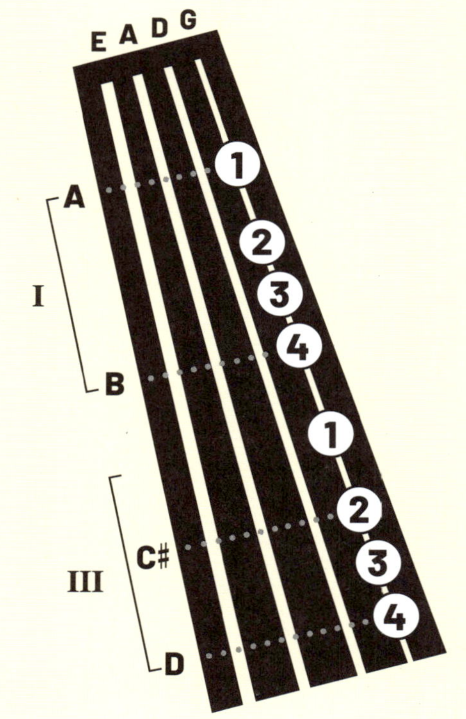

Listening Skills Play what your teacher plays. Listen carefully.

THEORY

Ledger Lines

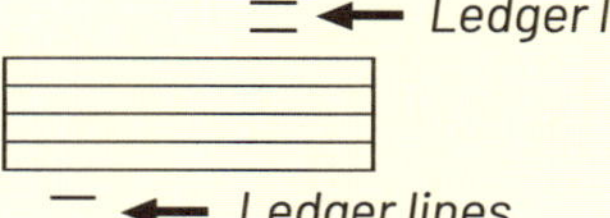

Ledger lines extend the music staff higher or lower.

23. LET'S READ "D"

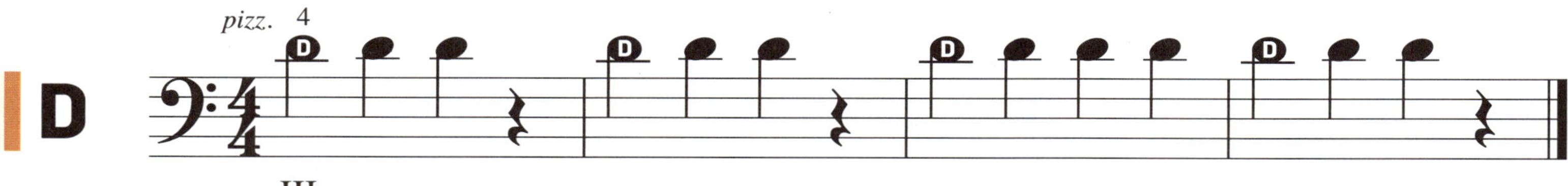

24. LET'S READ "C♯" (C-sharp)

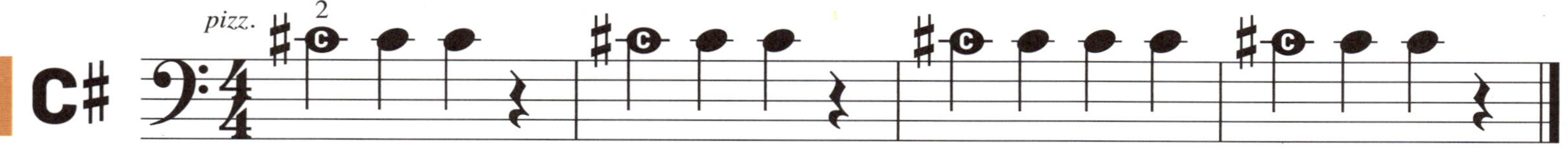

▲ *Play all C♯'s. Sharps apply to the entire measure.*

25. TAKE OFF

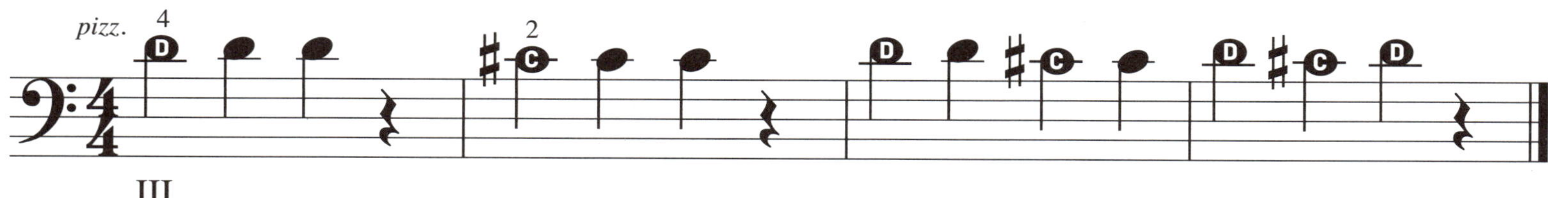

26. CARIBBEAN ISLAND

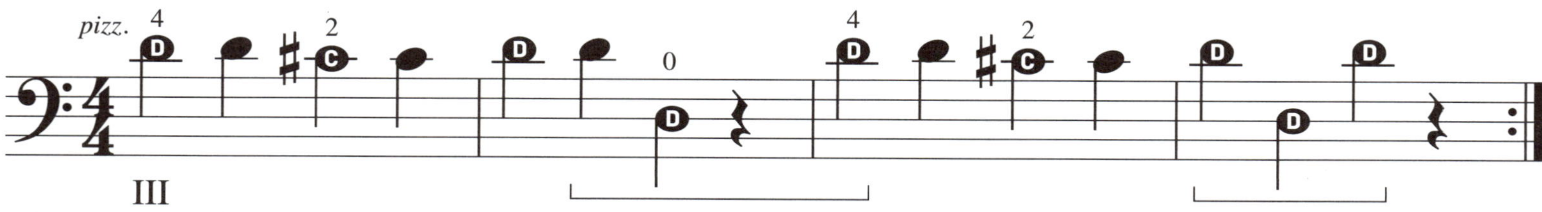

★ Practice BOW BUILDERS ONE, TWO, and THREE daily.

27. OLYMPIC HIGH JUMP

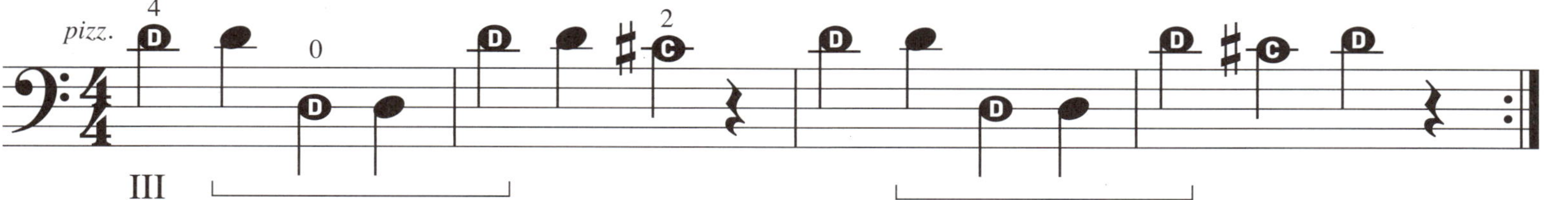

28. LET'S READ "B"

B

Shifting Sliding your left hand smoothly and lightly to a new location on the fingerboard, indicated by a dash (–).

29. HALF WAY DOWN

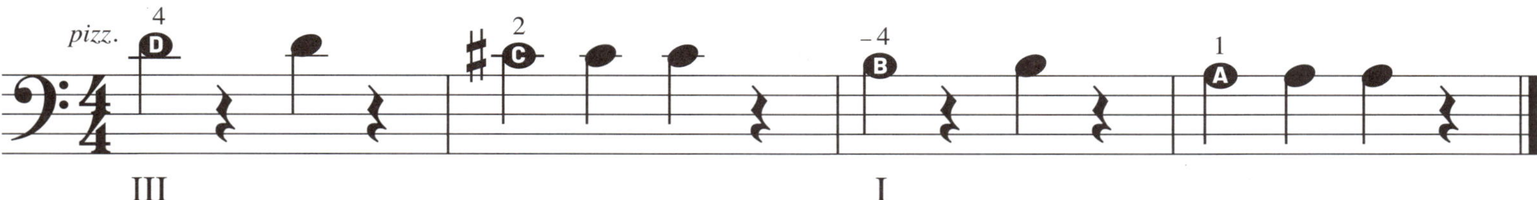

30. RIGHT BACK UP

Scale A **scale** is a sequence of notes in ascending or descending order. Like a musical "ladder," each note is the next consecutive step of the scale. This is your D Scale. The first and last notes are both D.

THEORY

31. DOWN THE D SCALE *Remember to memorize the note names.*

32. ESSENTIAL ELEMENTS QUIZ – UP THE D SCALE

BOW BUILDER FOUR

On the Bow *(French)*

Step 1 Identify all parts of the bow (see page 2). Hold the bow in your left hand near the tip with the frog pointing to the right.

Step 2 Place the bow between your right thumb and second finger. The tip of your thumb will contact the stick next to the frog, and your second finger will extend to the ferrule.

Step 3 Shape the remaining fingers on the bow stick as shown.

Step 4 Turn your right hand over, and be sure your thumb is curved.

Step 5 Hold the bow and repeat the exercises on page 8.

On the Bow *(German)* 

Step 1 Identify all parts of the bow (see page 2). Hold the bow in your left hand near the tip with the frog pointing to the right.

Step 2 Place the frog in your right hand at the base joints of your fingers.

Step 3 Put your thumb on top of the bow while the tips of the first and second fingers touch the side of the stick and frog.

Step 4 Hook your fourth finger underneath the frog touching the ferrule. Allow the third finger to curve and relax.

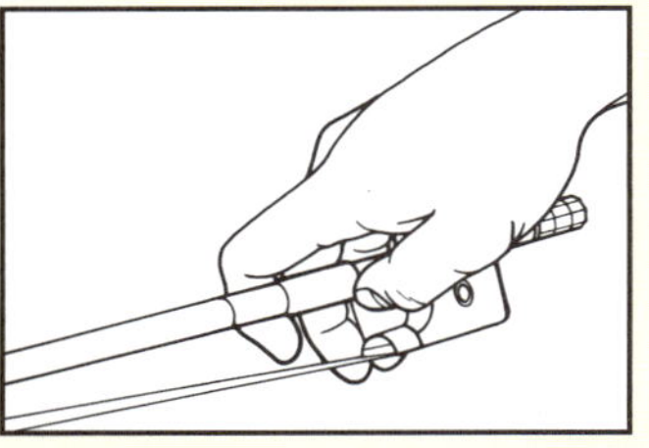
French Bow

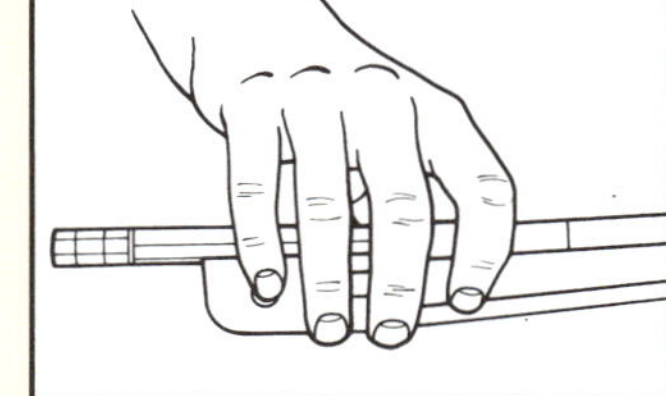
French Bow

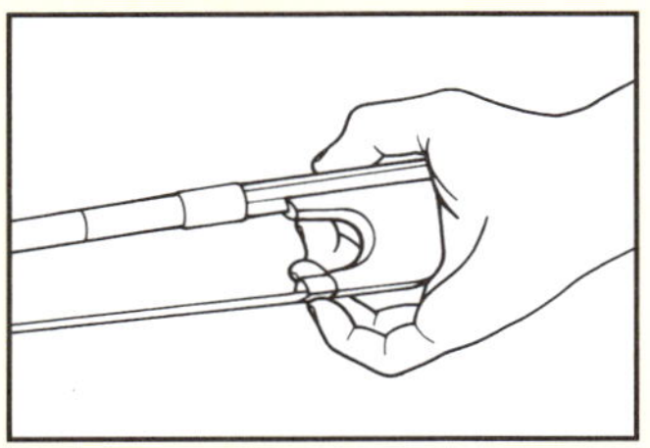
German Bow

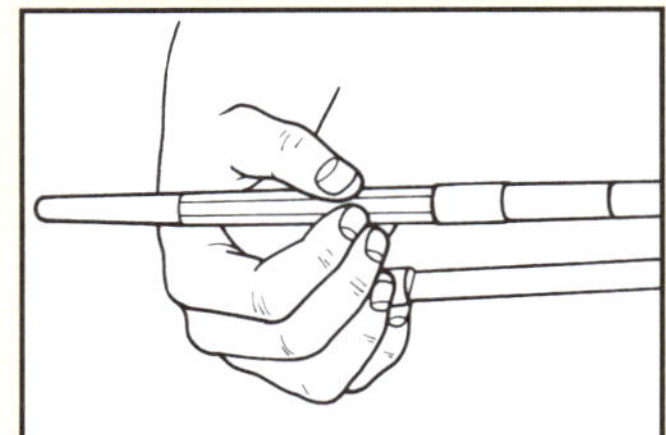
German Bow

Alert Do not place your bow on the instrument until instructed to do so by your teacher.

33. SONG FOR CHRISTINE

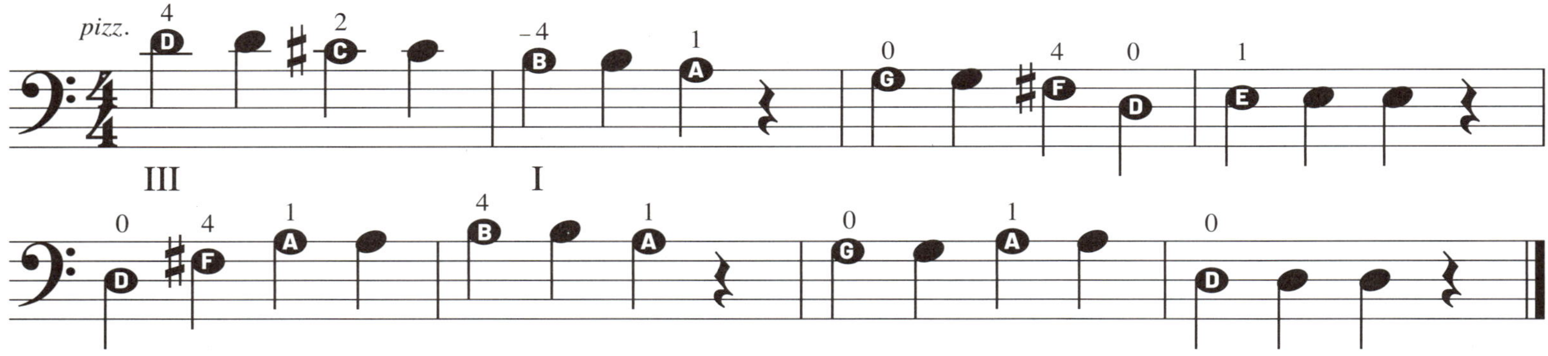

34. NATALIE'S ROSE *Remember to count.*

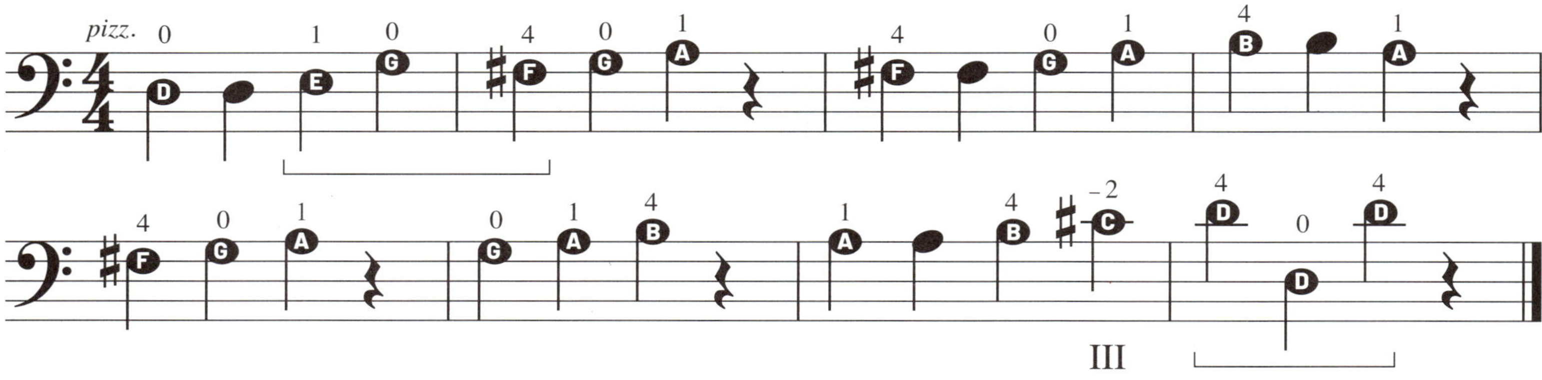

35. ESSENTIAL CREATIVITY *How many words can you create by drawing notes on the staff below?*

Folk songs often tell stories. This **Israeli folk song** describes a game played with a dreidel, a small table-top spinning toy that has been enjoyed by families for centuries. The game is especially popular in December around the time of Hanukkah.

36. DREIDEL

Israeli Folk Song

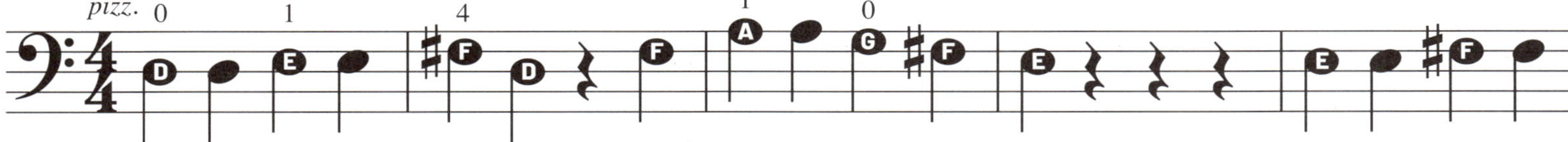

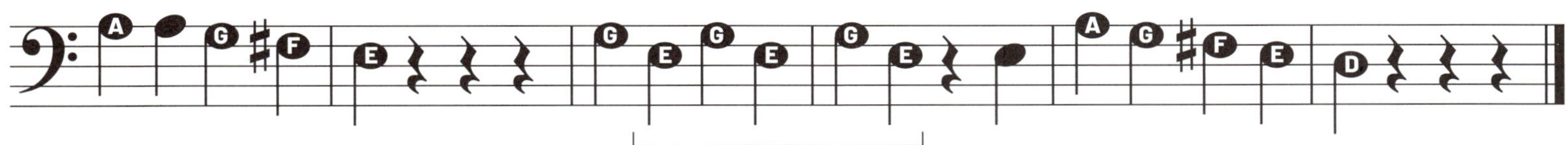

BOW BUILDER FIVE

Shadow Bowing

Shadow Bowing is bowing without the instrument.

Step 1 Tighten the bow hair as instructed by your teacher.

Step 2 Place the rosin in your left hand. Hold the bow in your right hand.

Step 3 Shadow bow by slowly moving the bow back and forth on the rosin. Be sure to move the bow, not the rosin.

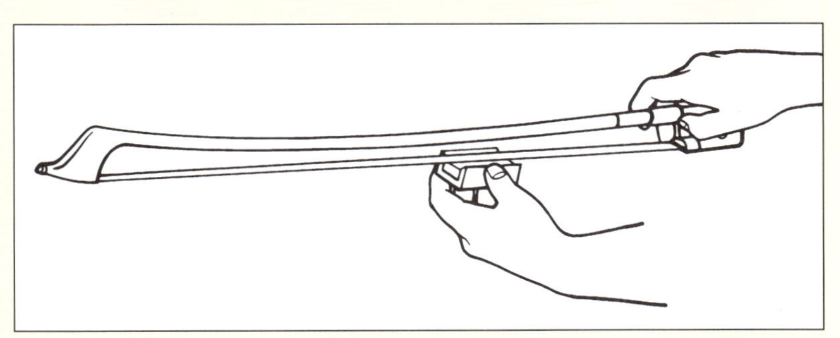

Down Bow ⊓ Move the bow away from your body (to the right).

Up Bow V Move the bow toward your body (to the left).

37. ROSIN RAP #1 *Bow these exercises on the rosin.*

38. ROSIN RAP #2

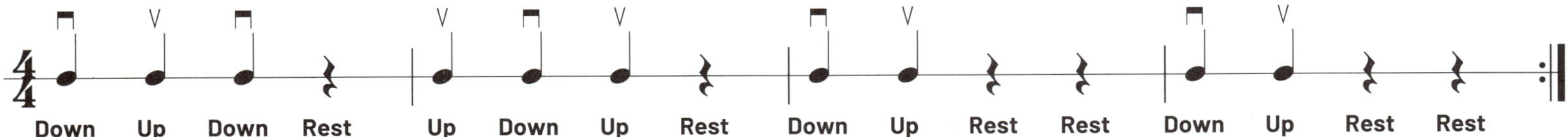

39. ROSIN RAP #3

✔ Is your bow hand shaped as shown in the diagram above?

40. CAROLINA BREEZE

41. JINGLE BELLS

J. S. Pierpont

42. OLD MACDONALD HAD A FARM

American Folk Song

★ Practice BOW BUILDER FIVE daily.

HISTORY

Austrian composer **Wolfgang Amadeus Mozart** (1756–1791) was a child prodigy who first performed in concert at age 6. He lived during the time of the American Revolution (1775–1783). Mozart's music is melodic and imaginative. He wrote hundreds of compositions, including a piano piece based on this familiar song.

43. A MOZART MELODY

Adapted by W. A. Mozart

THEORY

Key Signature D MAJOR

A **key signature** tells us what notes to play with sharps and flats throughout the entire piece. Play all F's as F♯ (F-sharp) and all C's as C♯ (C-sharp) when you see this key signature, which is called "D Major."

44. MATTHEW'S MARCH

45. CHRISTOPHER'S TUNE

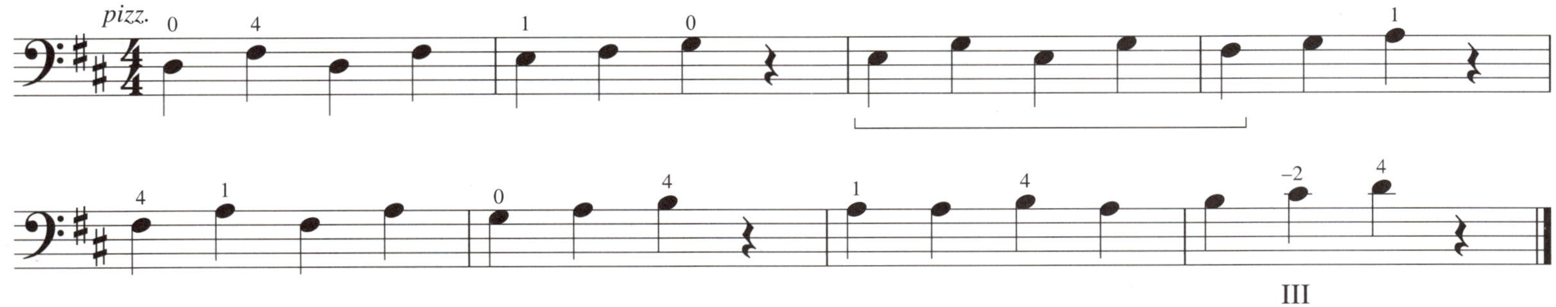

46. ESSENTIAL CREATIVITY

Play the notes below. Then compose your own music for the last two measures using the notes you have learned with this rhythm:

BOW BUILDER SIX

Let's Bow!

French Bow Hold

German Bow Hold

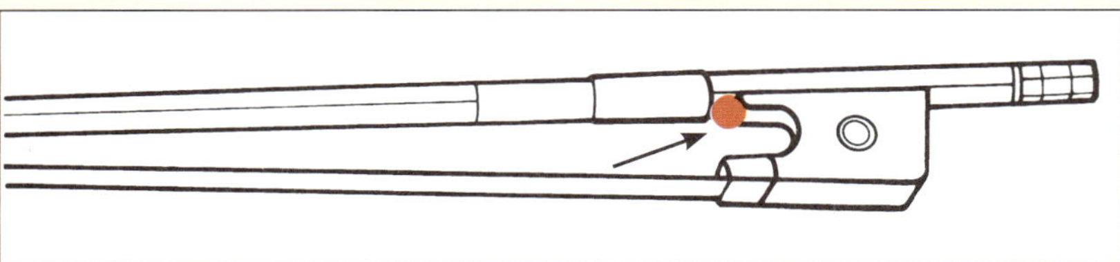

Thumb Placement (French)

Listening Skills Play what your teacher plays. Listen carefully. Your tone should be smooth and even.

47. BOW ON THE D STRING

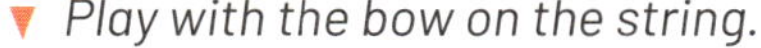

Play with the bow on the string.

arco

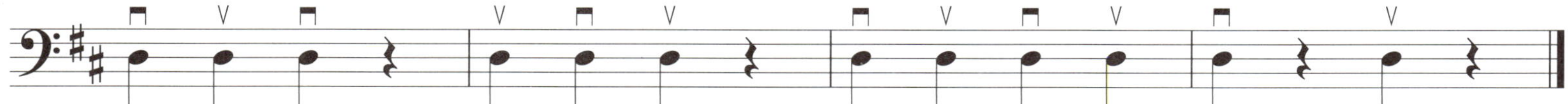

48. BOW ON THE A STRING

WORKOUTS

String Levels

Your arm moves when bowing on different strings. Memorize these guidelines:

- Move your arm **forward** and **up** to play **higher**-pitched strings.
- Move your arm **back** and **down** to play **lower**-pitched strings.

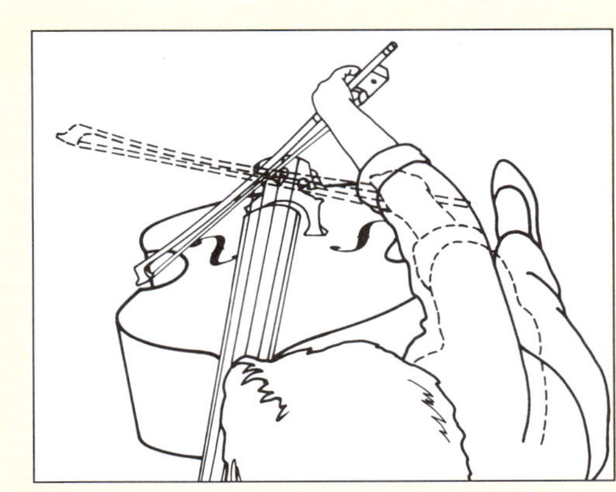

Raise arm = higher string

Lower arm = lower string

49. RAISE AND LOWER

50. TEETER TOTTER

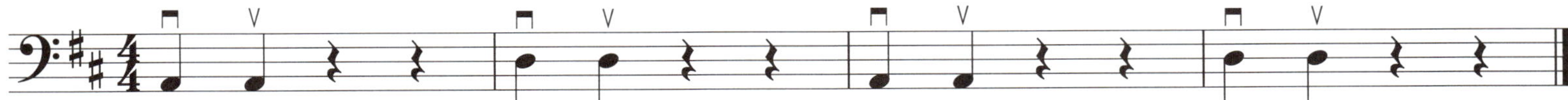

51. MIRROR IMAGE

Bow Lift

Lift the bow and return to its starting point.

52. A STRAND OF D 'N' A

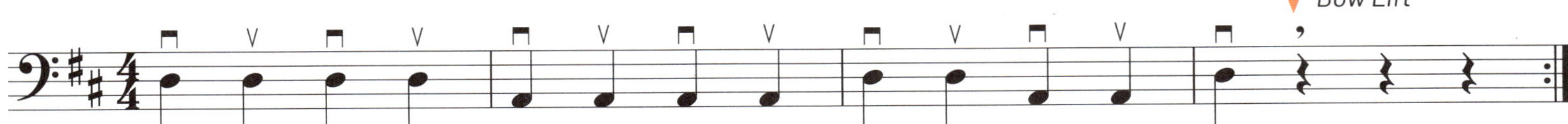

53. ESSENTIAL ELEMENTS QUIZ – OLYMPIC CHALLENGE

BOW BUILDER SEVEN

Combining Both Hands

Using notes from the D major scale, echo what your teacher plays.

PUTTING IT ALL TOGETHER

Congratulations! You are now ready to practice like an advanced player by combining left and right hand skills while reading music. When learning a new line of music, follow these steps for success:

Step 1 Tap your toe and say or sing the letter names.

Step 2 Play *pizz.* and say or sing the letter names.

Step 3 Shadow bow and say or sing the letter names.

Step 4 Bow and play as written.

54. BOWING "G"

55. BACK AND FORTH

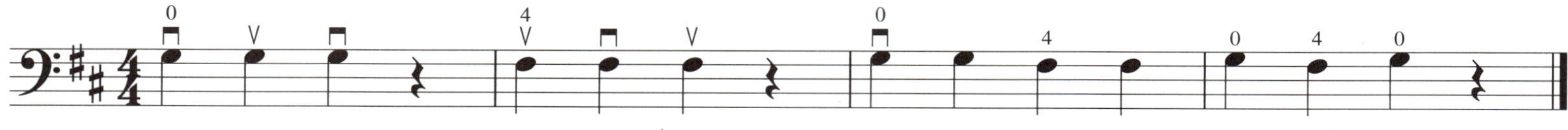

56. DOWN AND UP

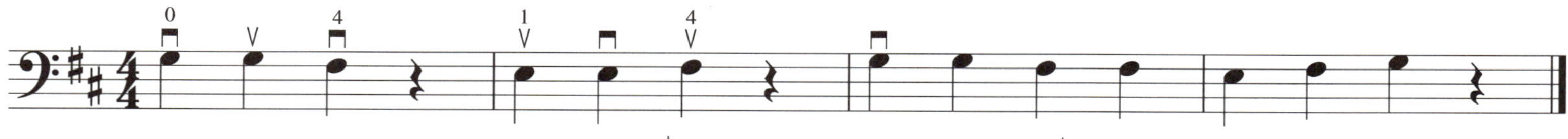

57. TRIBAL LAMENT

58. BOWING "D"

59. LITTLE STEPS

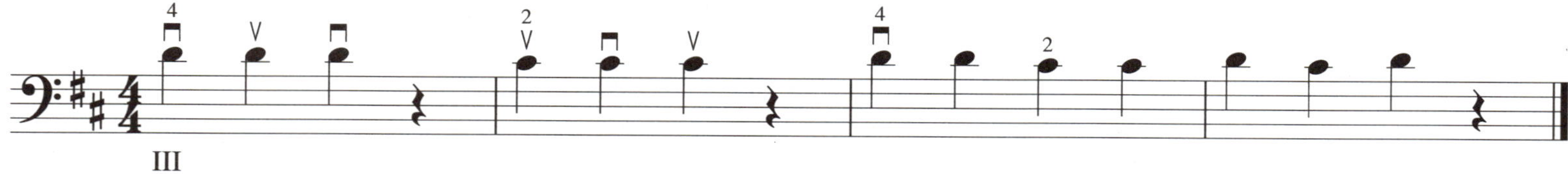

60. ELEVATOR DOWN

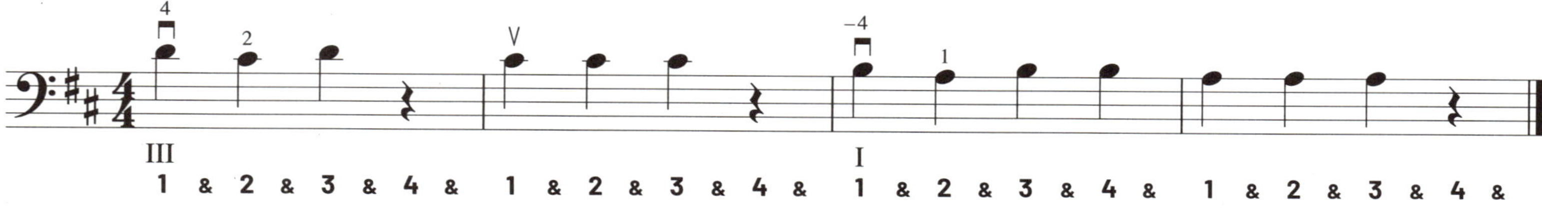

61. ELEVATOR UP

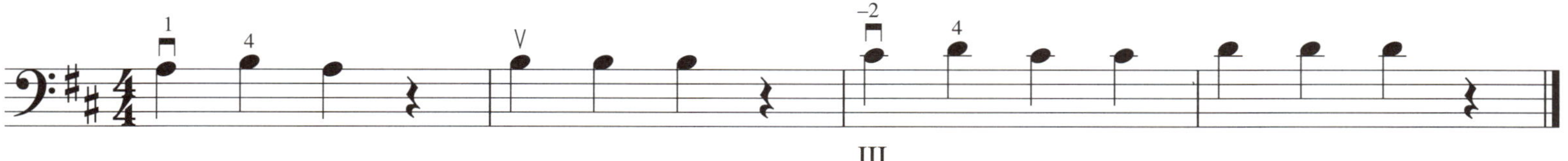

62. DOWN THE D MAJOR SCALE

63. SCALE SIMULATOR *Remember to count.*

64. ESSENTIAL ELEMENTS QUIZ – THE D MAJOR SCALE

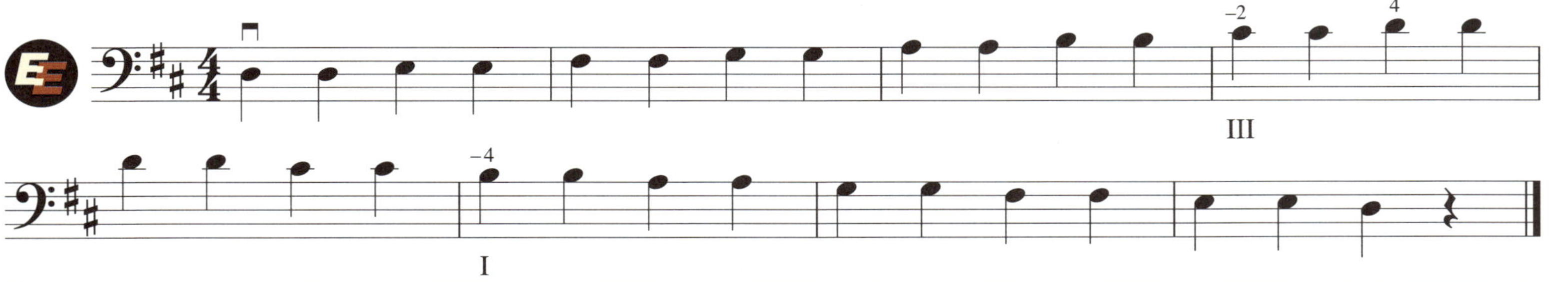

C♯

is played with 4 fingers on the A string.

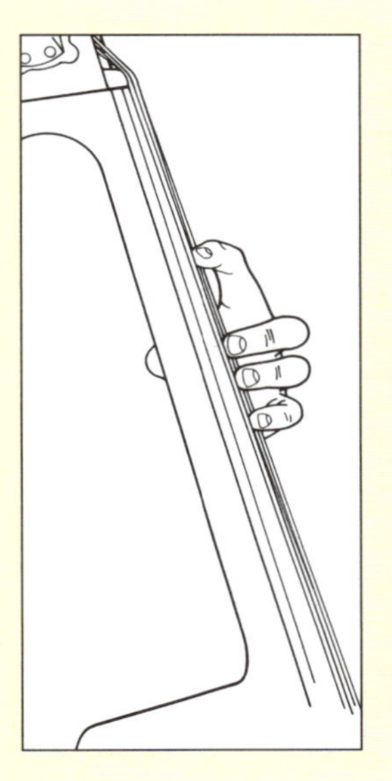

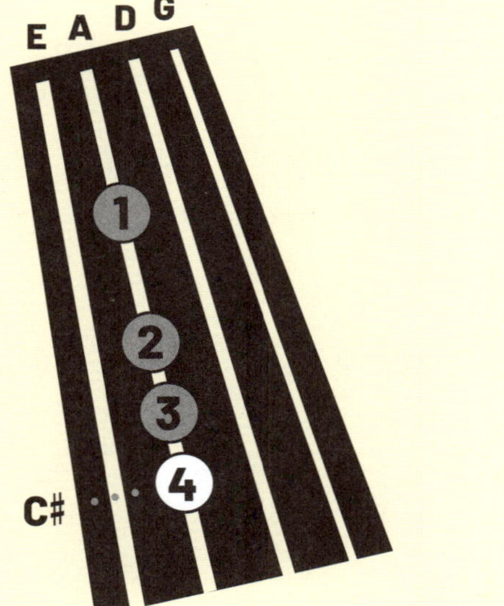

65. LET'S READ "C♯" – Review

THEORY

Eighth Notes

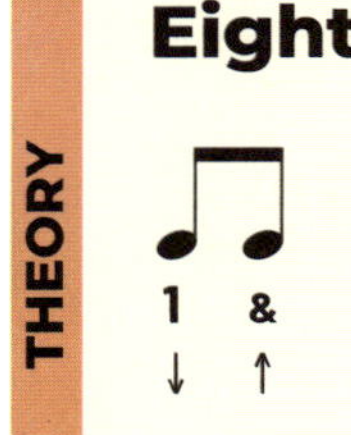

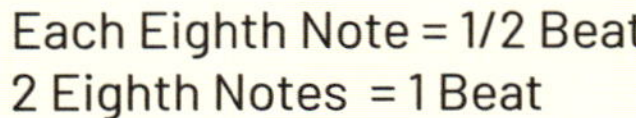

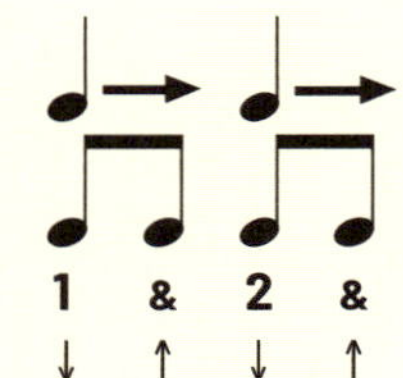

Two or more Eighth Notes have a *beam* across the stems.

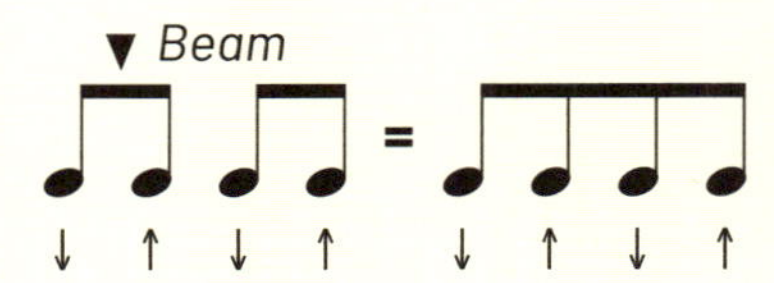

Tap your toe down on the number and up on the "&."

66. RHYTHM RAP

Shadow bow and count before playing.

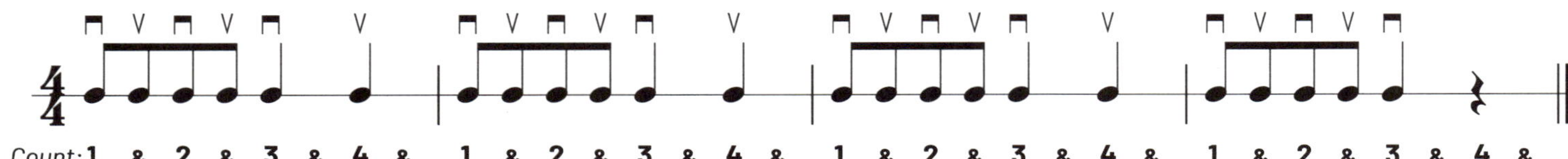

67. PEPPERONI PIZZA

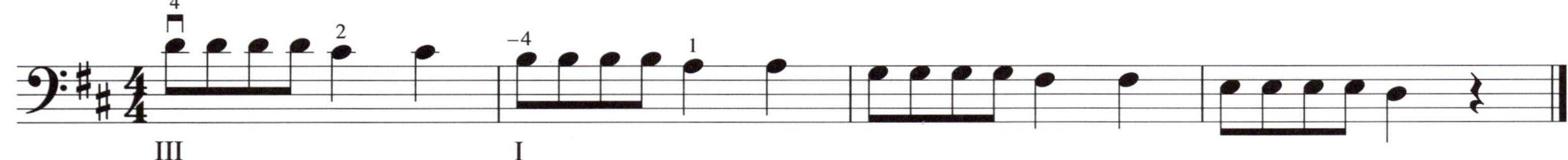

68. RHYTHM RAP

Shadow bow and count before playing.

69. D MAJOR SCALE UP

Tempo Markings

Tempo is the speed of music. Tempo markings are usually written above the staff, in Italian.

Allegro – Fast tempo **Moderato** – Medium tempo **Andante** – Slower, walking tempo

70. HOT CROSS BUNS

Moderato

71. AU CLAIRE DE LA LUNE

French Folk Song

Andante

72. RHYTHM RAP

Shadow bow and count before playing.

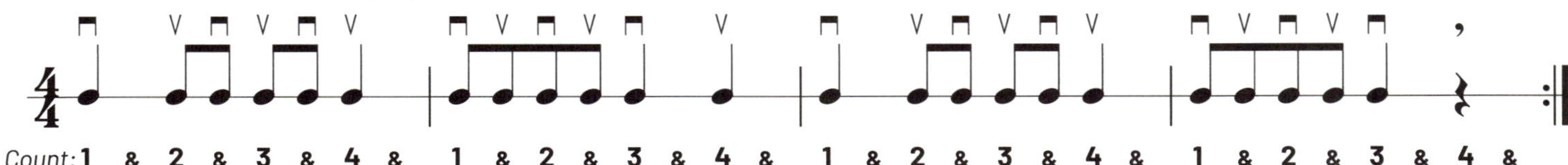

73. BUCKEYE SALUTE

Time Signature

= **2 beats** per measure
= **Quarter** note gets one beat

Conducting

Practice conducting this two-beat pattern.

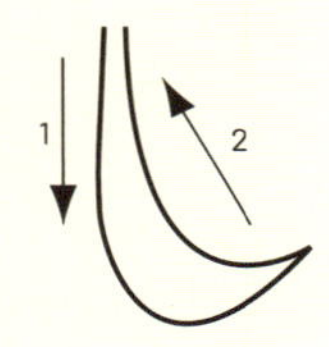

THEORY

74. RHYTHM RAP

Shadow bow and count before playing.

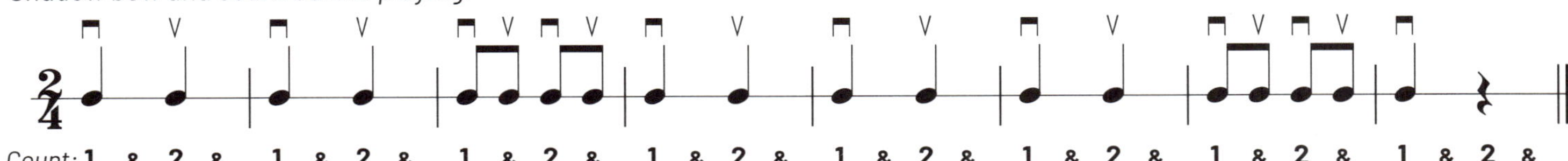

75. TWO BY TWO

1st & 2nd Endings

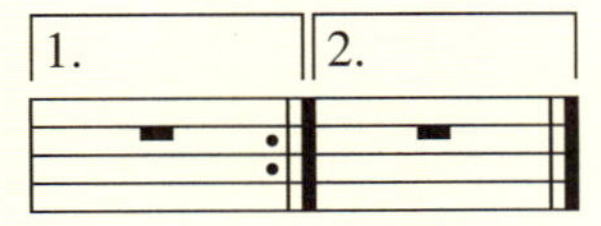

Play the 1st ending the 1st time through. Then, repeat the same section of music, skip the 1st ending, and play the 2nd ending.

THEORY

76. ESSENTIAL ELEMENTS QUIZ – FOR PETE'S SAKE

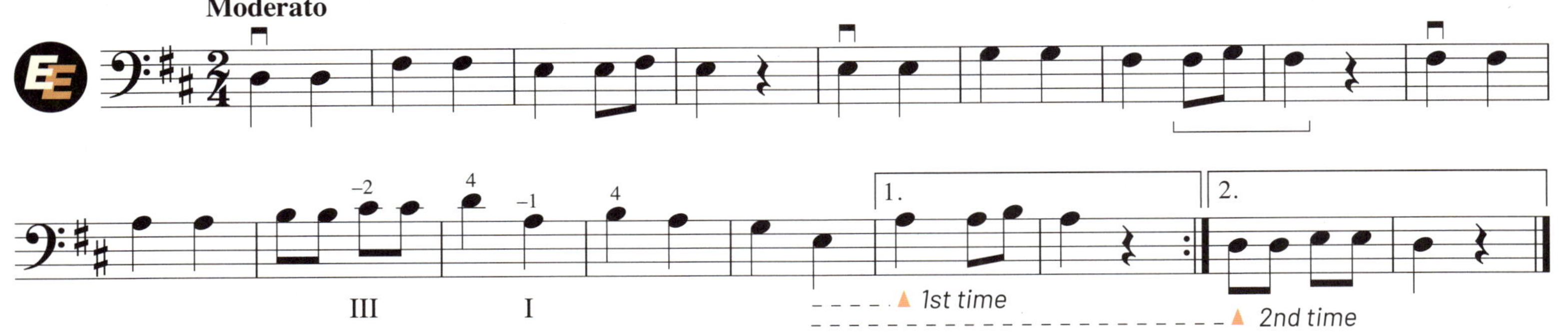

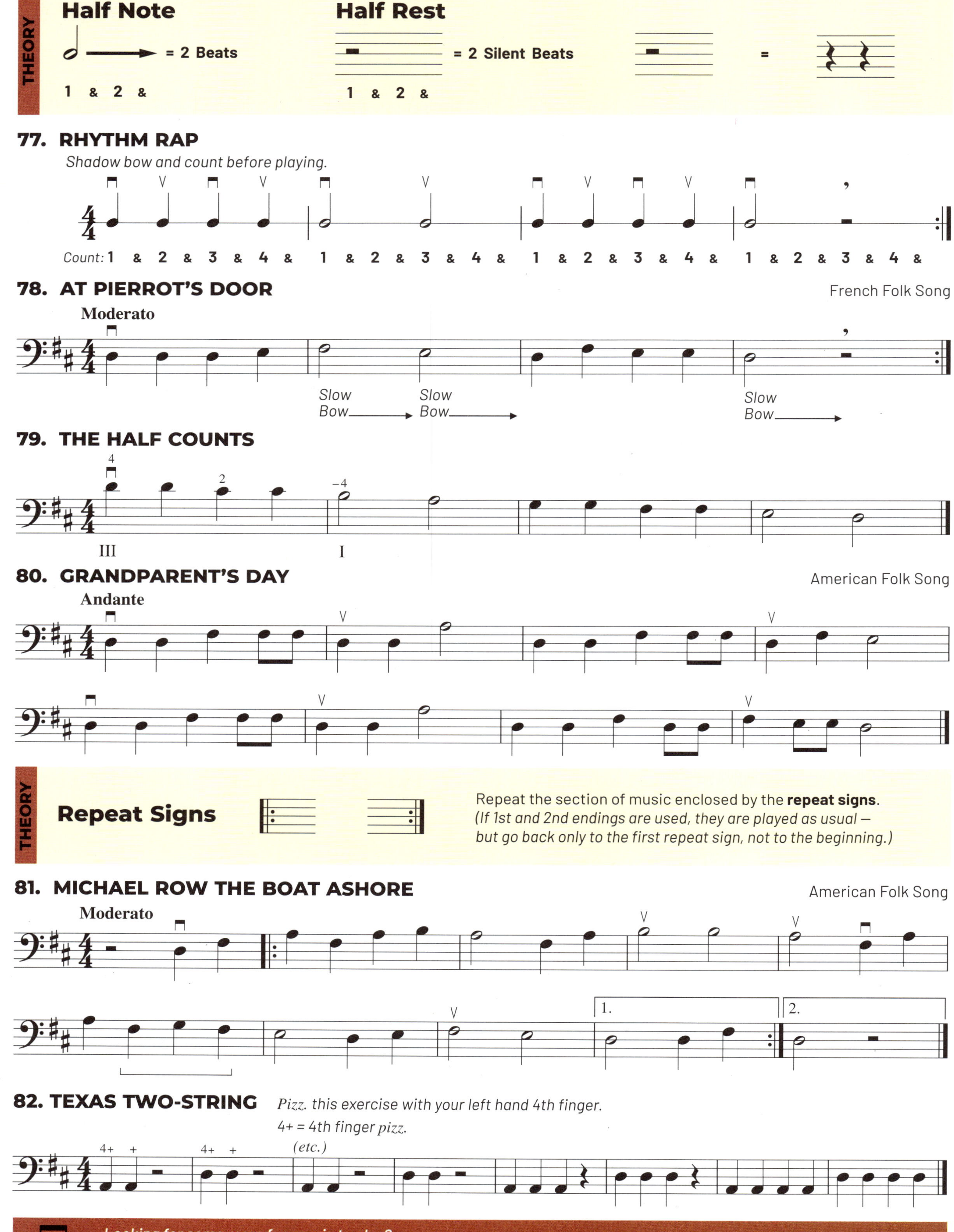
THEORY
Half Note
= 2 Beats
1 & 2 &
Half Rest
= 2 Silent Beats
1 & 2 &
=
77. RHYTHM RAP
Shadow bow and count before playing.
Count: 1 & 2 & 3 & 4 & 1 & 2 & 3 & 4 & 1 & 2 & 3 & 4 & 1 & 2 & 3 & 4 &
78. AT PIERROT'S DOOR
French Folk Song
Moderato
Slow Bow
Slow Bow
Slow Bow
79. THE HALF COUNTS
III
I
80. GRANDPARENT'S DAY
American Folk Song
Andante
THEORY
Repeat Signs
Repeat the section of music enclosed by the **repeat signs**.
(If 1st and 2nd endings are used, they are played as usual — but go back only to the first repeat sign, not to the beginning.)
81. MICHAEL ROW THE BOAT ASHORE
American Folk Song
Moderato
1.
2.
82. TEXAS TWO-STRING
Pizz. this exercise with your left hand 4th finger.
4+ = 4th finger *pizz.*
(etc.)
Looking for some more fun music to play?
See the inside front cover for instructions on accessing recent popular Bonus Songs.

NEW NOTES

A is played with 4 fingers on the D string in third position (III).

G is played with 1 finger on the D string in third position (III).

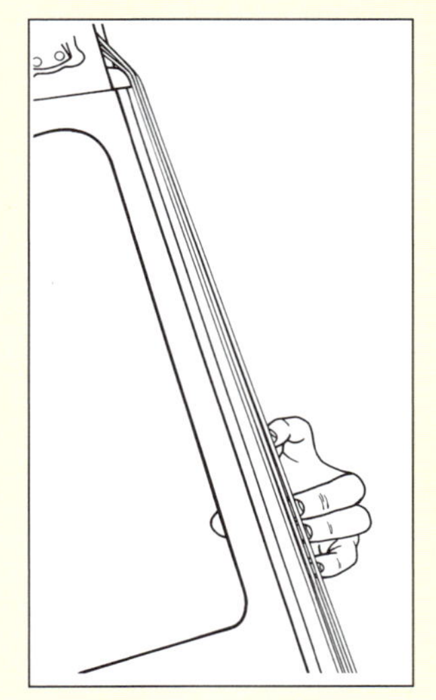

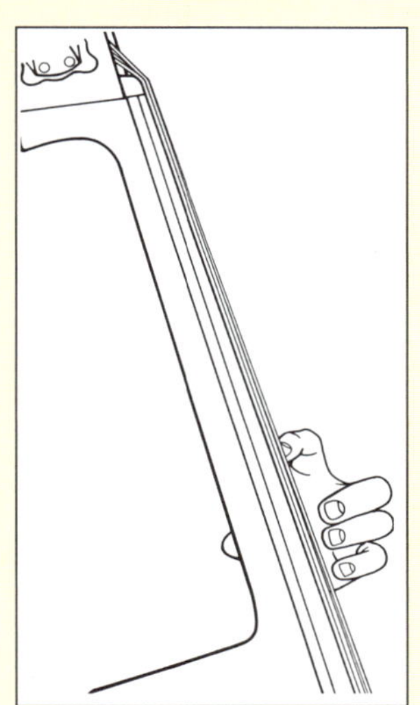

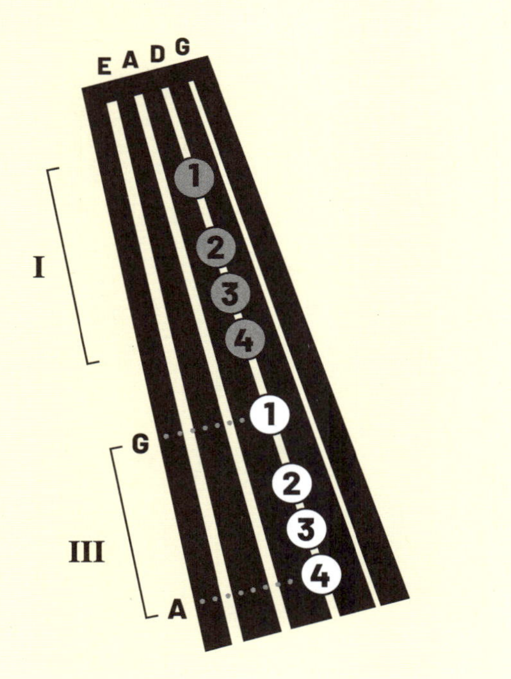

83. FOUR BY FOUR

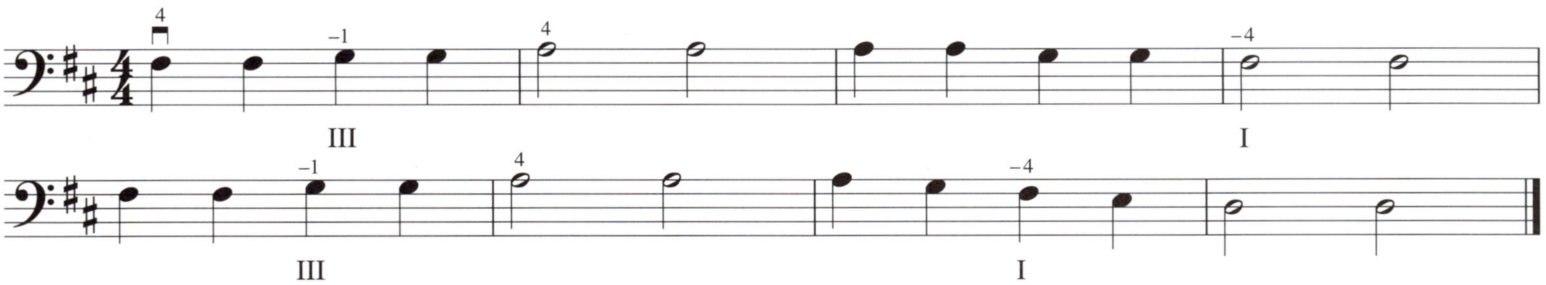

84. 4TH FINGER MARATHON

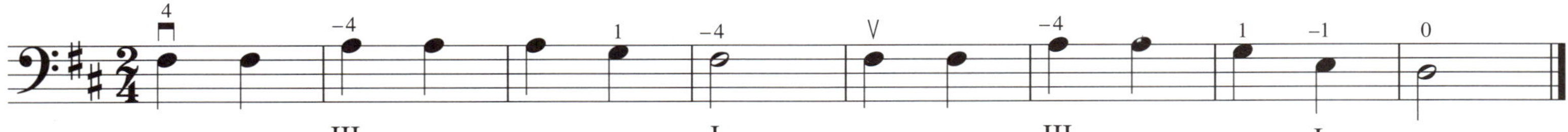

85. HIGH FLYING

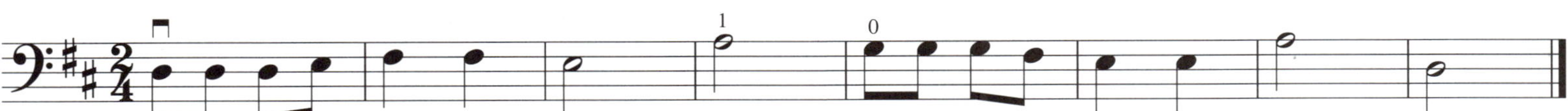

German composer **Ludwig van Beethoven** (1770–1827) was one of the world's greatest composers. He was completely deaf by 1802. Although he could not hear music like we do, he could "hear" it in his mind. The theme of his final *Symphony No. 9* is called "Ode To Joy," and was written to the text of a poem by Friedrich von Schiller. "Ode To Joy" was featured in concerts celebrating the reunification of Germany in 1990.

HISTORY

86. ESSENTIAL ELEMENTS QUIZ – ODE TO JOY

Ludwig van Beethoven

PERFORMANCE SPOTLIGHT

Good performers are on time with their instruments and music ready, dressed appropriately, and know their music well.

87. SCALE WARM-UP

88. FRÈRE JACQUES – Round *(When group A reaches ②, group B begins at ①)*

French Folk Song

Moderato

THEORY

Chord, Harmony

Two or more pitches sounding at the same time form a **chord** or **harmony**. Throughout this book, **A** = Melody and **B** = Harmony.

89. BOIL 'EM CABBAGE DOWN – Orchestra Arrangement

American Fiddle Tune

Allegro

PERFORMANCE SPOTLIGHT

90. ENGLISH ROUND

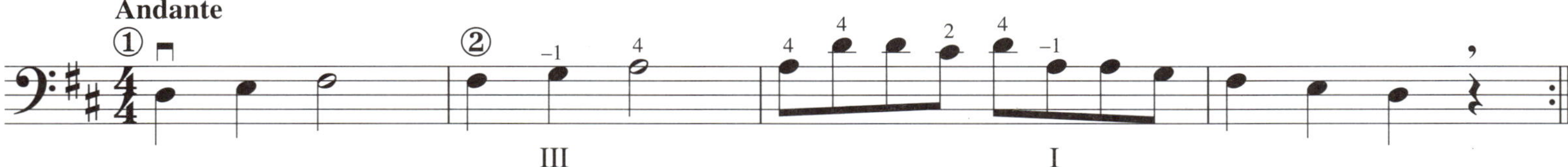

91. LIGHTLY ROW – Orchestra Arrangement

HISTORY

French composer **Jacques Offenbach** (1819–1880) was the originator of the **operetta** and played the cello. An **operetta** is a form of entertainment that combines several of the fine arts together: vocal and instrumental music, drama, dance, and visual arts. One of his most famous pieces is the "Can-Can" dance from *Orpheus And The Underworld*. This popular work was written in 1858, just three years before the start of the American Civil War (1861–1865).

92. CAN-CAN – Orchestra Arrangement

Jacques Offenbach
Arr. John Higgins

✔ What were the strong points of your performance?

NEW NOTES – E AND A STRINGS

G is played with 2 fingers on the E string.

C is played with 2 fingers on the A string.

B is played with 1 finger on the A string.

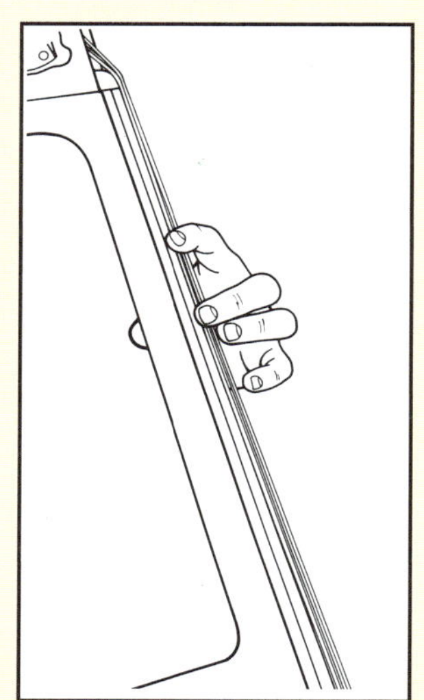

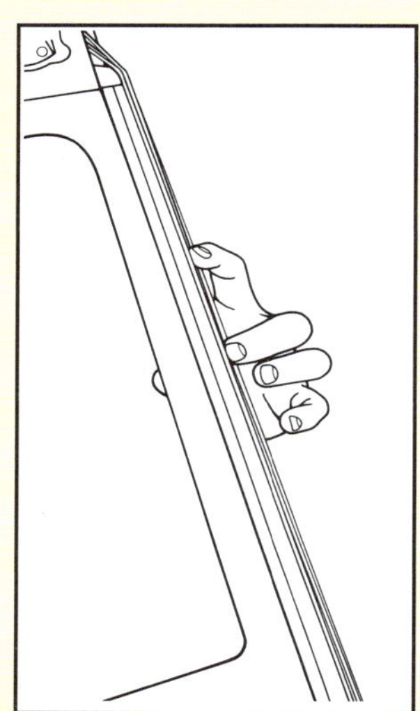

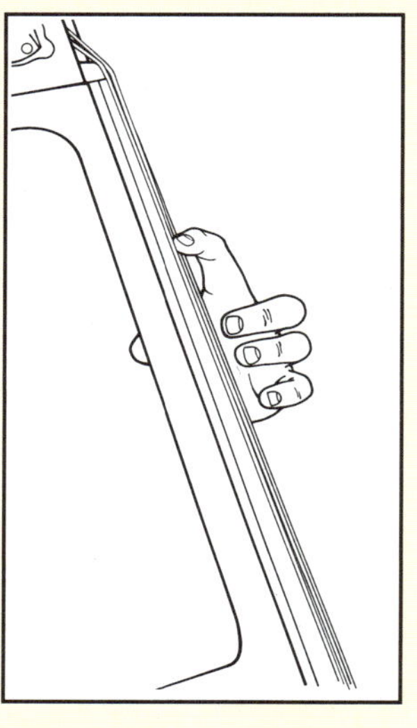

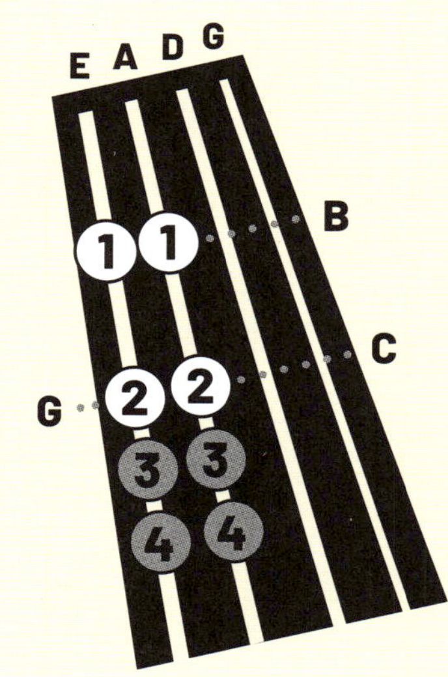

Listening Skills Play what your teacher plays. Listen carefully.

Key Signature G MAJOR

Play all F's as F♯ (F-sharp) and all C's as C♮ (C-natural).

93. LET'S READ "G"

▲ *Play F♯'s and C♮'s in this key signature.*

94. LET'S READ "C" (C-natural)

95. LET'S READ "B"

96. LET'S READ "A"

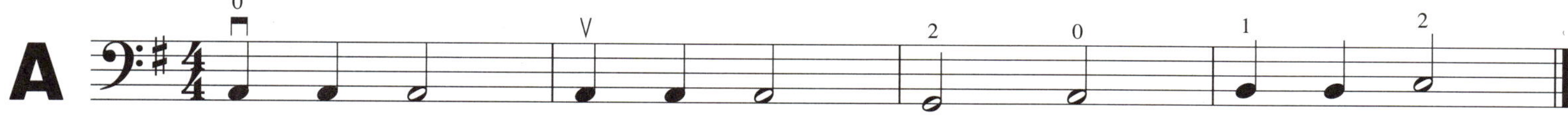

97. WALKING AROUND *Name the notes before you play.*

98. G MAJOR SCALE *Write the note names before you play.*

99. FOURTH FINGER D *(for violins and violas)*

Time Signature *(Meter)*

C = **Common Time** (Same as 4/4)

Conducting

Practice conducting this four-beat pattern.

THEORY

100. LOW DOWN

101. BAA BAA BLACK SHEEP

Moderato

102. ESSENTIAL ELEMENTS QUIZ – THIS OLD MAN

American Folk Song

Moderato

THEORY
Time Signature
(Meter)
3 = 3 beats per measure
4 = ♩ or 𝄽 note gets one beat
Conducting
Practice conducting this three-beat pattern.
1
2
3
Dotted Half Note
= 3 Beats of Sound
1 & 2 & 3 &
Dot
A dot adds half the value of the note.
2 beats + 1 beat = 3 beats
103. RHYTHM RAP
Shadow bow and count before playing.
Count: 1 & 2 & 3 & 1 & 2 & 3 & 1 & 2 & 3 & 1 & 2 & 3 &
104. COUNTING THREES
Slow Bow
Slow Bow
105. D MAJOR SCALE IN THREES
III
I
New Position – II½
(Second and a half position – first finger on B.)
106. FRENCH FOLK SONG
French Folk Song
Moderato
III
II½
III
I
III
I
107. ESSENTIAL ELEMENTS QUIZ – SAILOR'S SONG
English Sea Song
Allegro
Write in the correct time signature before you begin.

Tie

A **tie** is a curved line that connects notes of the **same** pitch. Play a single note for the combined counts of the tied notes.

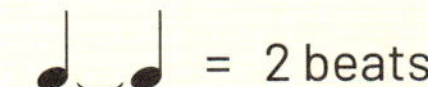

THEORY

108. FIT TO BE TIED

Slur

A **slur** is a curved line that connects two or more **different** pitches. Play slurred notes together in the same bow stroke.

THEORY

109. STOP AND GO

110. SLURRING ALONG

111. SMOOTH SAILING

112. D MAJOR SLURS

113. CROSSING STRINGS

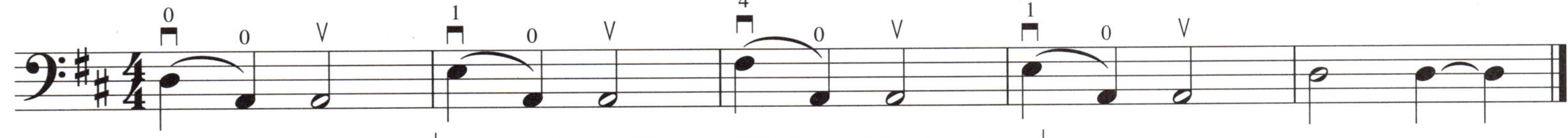

114. GLIDING BOWS

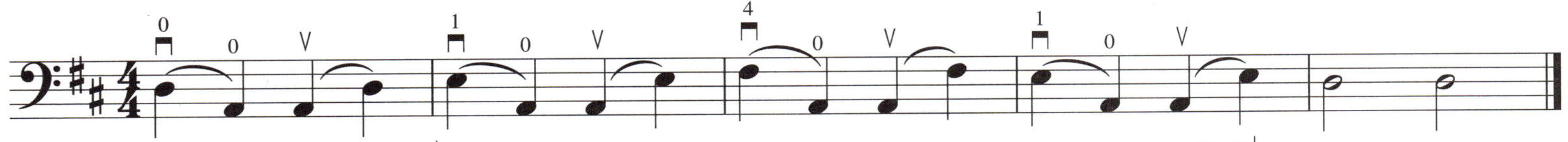

115. UPSIDE DOWN

THEORY

Upbeat

A note (or notes) that appears before the first full measure is called an **upbeat** (or **pickup**). The remaining beats are found in the last measure.

116. SONG FOR MARIA

HISTORY

Latin American music combines the folk music from South and Central America, the Caribbean Islands, African, Spanish, and Portuguese cultures. Melodies often feature a lively accompaniment by drums, maracas, and claves. Latin American styles have become part of jazz, classical, and rock music.

THEORY

D.C. al Fine

Play until you see the **D.C. al Fine**. Then go back to the beginning and play until you see **Fine** (*fee'- nay*). **D.C.** is the abbreviation for **Da Capo**, the Italian term for "return to the beginning." **Fine** is the Italian word for "the finish."

117. BANANA BOAT SONG

Caribbean Folk Song

118. FIROLIRALERA – Orchestra Arrangement

Mexican Folk Song
Arr. John Higgins

SKILL BUILDERS – G Major

119.

120.

121.

122.

123.

Slur three

124.

Far Eastern music comes from Malaysia, Indonesia, China and other areas. Historians believe the first orchestras, known as **gamelans**, existed in this region as early as the 1st century B.C. Today's gamelans include rebabs (spiked fiddles), gongs, xylophones, and a wide variety of percussion instruments.

HISTORY

125. JINGLI NONA

Far Eastern Folk Song

SECOND FINGER ON THE D STRING

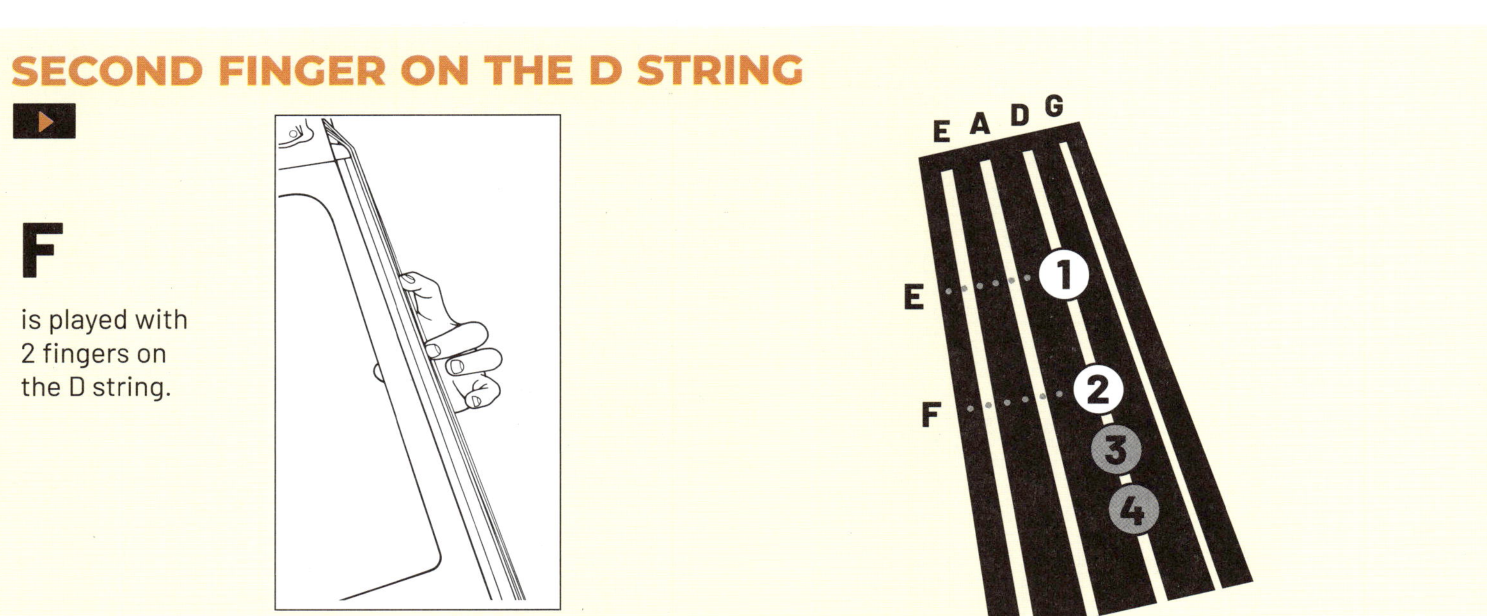

Listening Skills Play what your teacher plays. Listen carefully.

THEORY

Natural ♮

A **natural** sign cancels out a flat (♭) or a sharp (♯) and remains in effect for the entire measure.

126. LET'S READ "F" (F-natural)

THEORY

Half Step A **half step** is the smallest distance between two notes.

Whole Step A **whole step** is two half steps combined.

127. HALF-STEPPIN' AND WHOLE-STEPPIN'

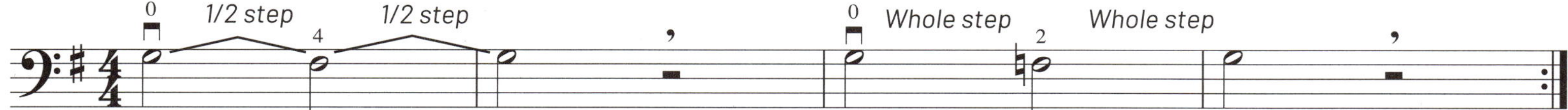

128. SPY GUY

129. MINOR DETAILS

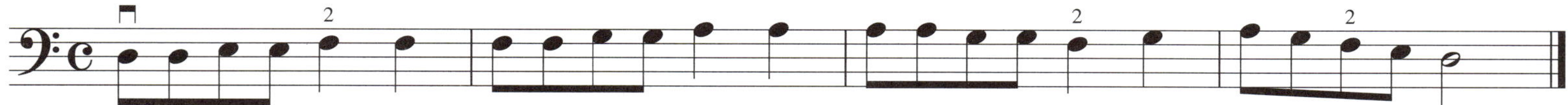

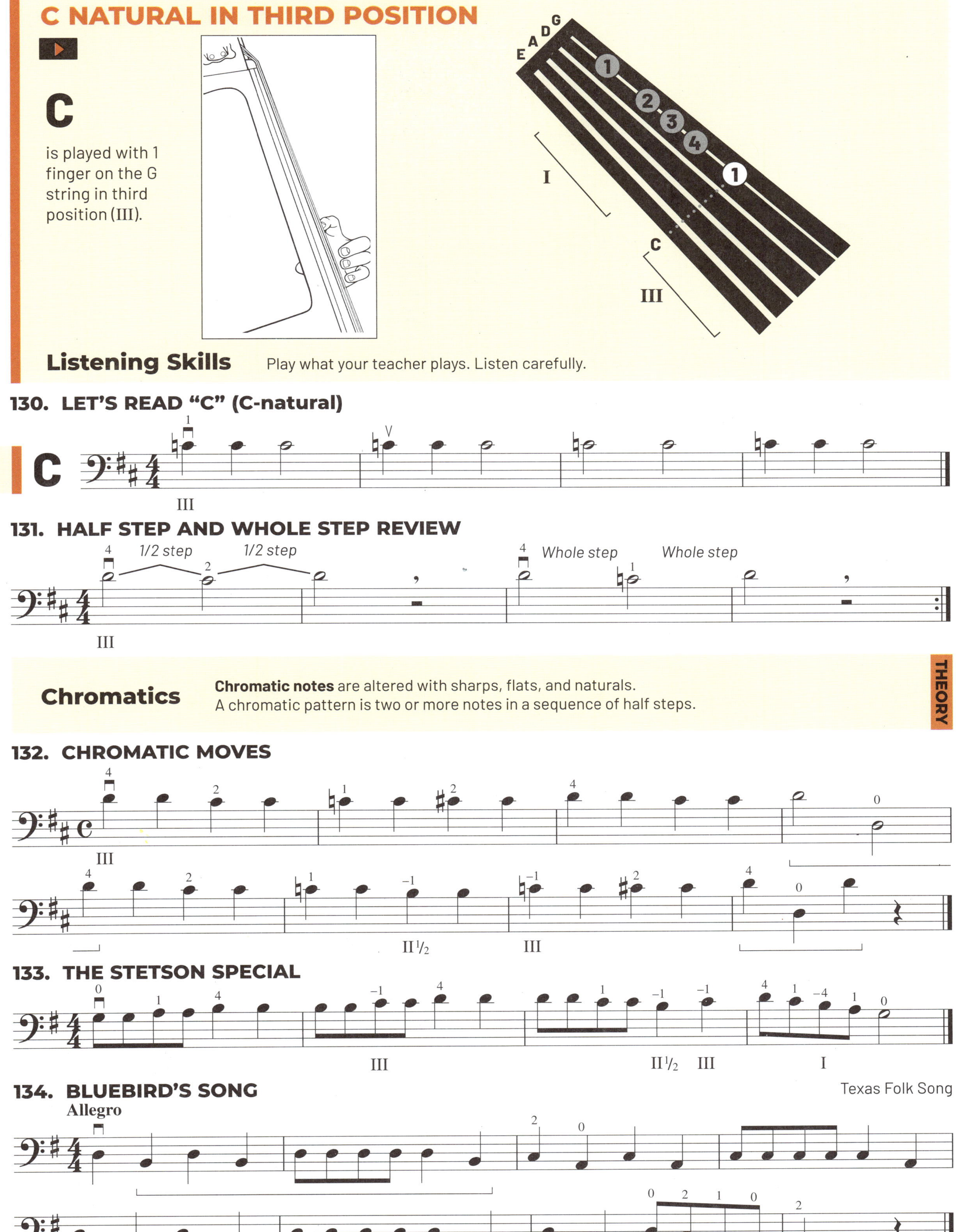
C NATURAL IN THIRD POSITION
C
is played with 1 finger on the G string in third position (III).
G D A E
1 2 3 4 1
I
C
III
Listening Skills
Play what your teacher plays. Listen carefully.
130. LET'S READ "C" (C-natural)
C
III
131. HALF STEP AND WHOLE STEP REVIEW
1/2 step
1/2 step
Whole step
Whole step
III
Chromatics
Chromatic notes are altered with sharps, flats, and naturals.
A chromatic pattern is two or more notes in a sequence of half steps.
THEORY
132. CHROMATIC MOVES
III
II½
III
133. THE STETSON SPECIAL
III
II½
III
I
134. BLUEBIRD'S SONG
Texas Folk Song
Allegro

THEORY

Key Signature C MAJOR All notes are naturals.

New Position – II (2nd finger on B, 4th finger on C.)

135. C MAJOR SCALE – Round

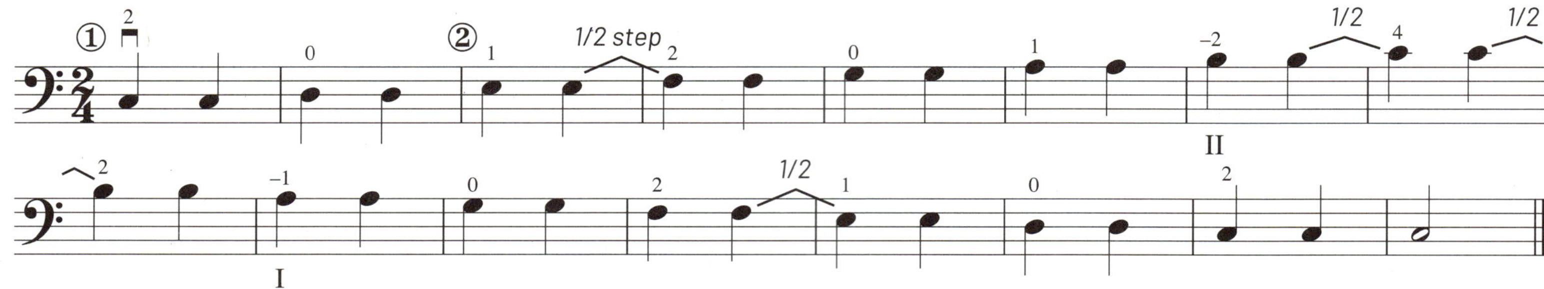

Duet A composition with two different parts, played together.

136. SPLIT DECISION – Duet

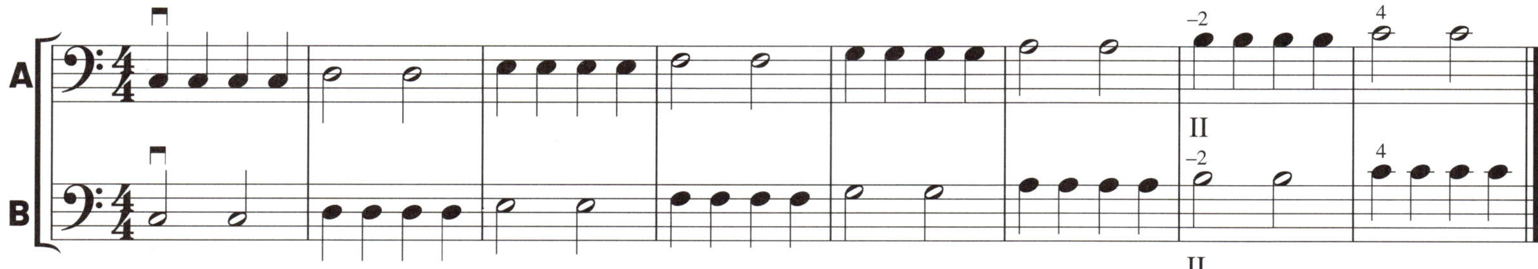

137. OAK HOLLOW

138. A-TISKET, A-TASKET

HISTORY

In the second half of the 1800s many composers tried to express the spirit of their own country by writing music with a distinct national flavor. Listen to the music of Russian composers such as Borodin, Tchaikovsky, and Rimsky-Korsakov. They often used folk songs and dance rhythms to convey their nationalism. Describe the sounds you hear.

139. ESSENTIAL ELEMENTS QUIZ – RUSSIAN FOLK TUNE

Russian Folk Song

Alert This page mixes finger patterns. *(For violins, violas, and cellos.)*

140. BINGO

18th Century English Game Song

Where is beat 2?

HISTORY

English composer **Thomas Tallis** (1505–1585) served as royal court composer during the reigns of Henry VIII, Edward VI, Mary, and Elizabeth I. Composers and artists during this era wanted to recreate the artistic and scientific glories of ancient Greece and Rome. The great artist Michelangelo painted the Sistine Chapel during Tallis' lifetime. **Rounds** and **canons** were popular forms of music during the early 16th century. Divide into groups, and play or sing the *Tallis Canon* as a 4-part round.

141. TALLIS CANON – Round

Thomas Tallis

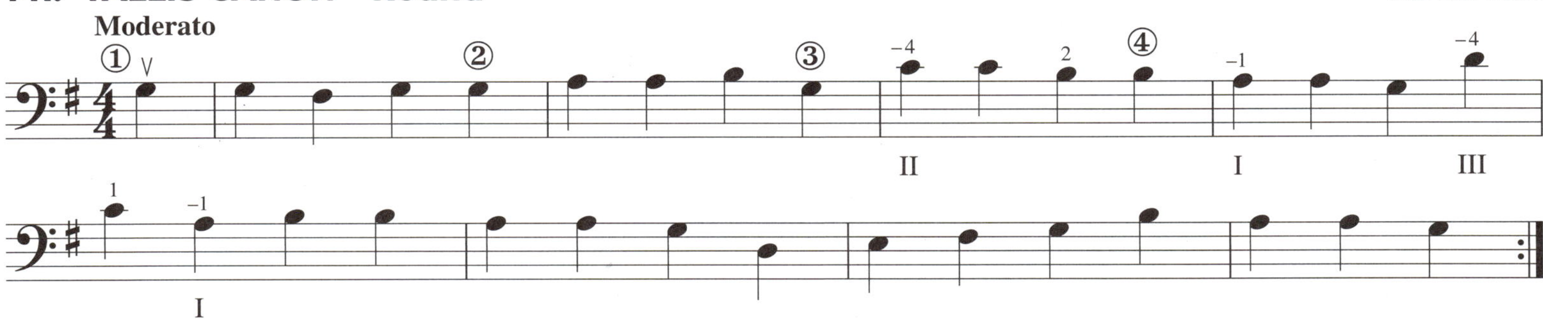

THEORY

Theme and Variations

Theme and Variations is a musical form where a theme, or melody, is followed by different versions of the same theme.

142. VARIATIONS ON A FAMILIAR SONG

Variation 2 – *make up your own variation*

143. ESSENTIAL CREATIVITY – THE BIRTHDAY SONG

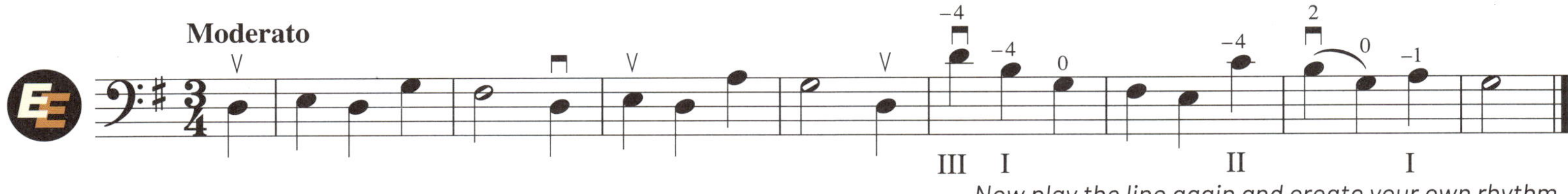

Now play the line again and create your own rhythm.

Special Double Bass Exercise

Write the note names below. Then, write stories using as many note names as possible. Share your work with orchestra friends.

Note Names: ___ ___ ___ ___ ___ ___ ___ ___ ___ ___ ___ ___ ___

___ ___ ___ ___ ___ ___ ___ ___ ___ ___ ___ ___ ___ ___

Team Work

Great musicians give encouragement to their fellow performers. Viola and cello players will now learn new challenging notes. The success of your orchestra depends on everyone's talent and patience. Play your best as these sections advance their musical technique.

Listening Skills

Play what your teacher plays. Listen carefully.

144. LET'S READ "C" – Review

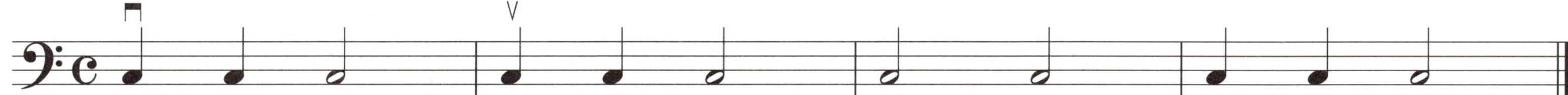

145. LET'S READ "F" – Review

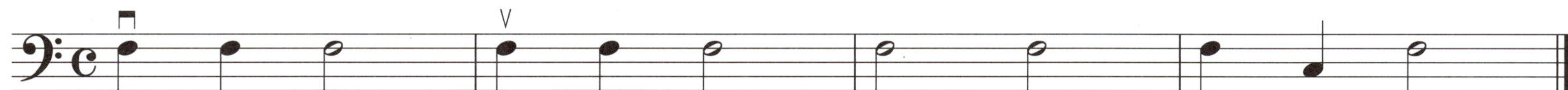

146. LET'S READ "E" – Review

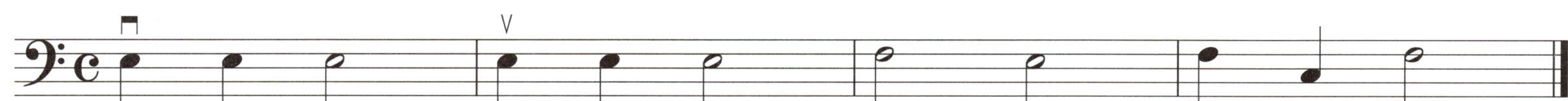

147. LET'S READ "D" – Review

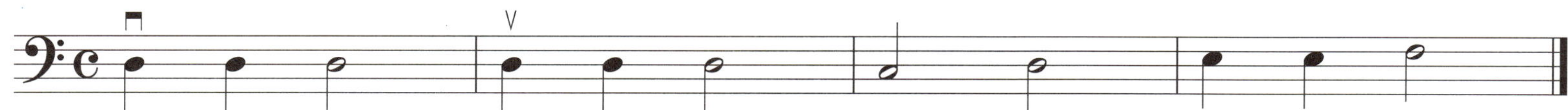

148. SIDE BY SIDE *Name the notes before you play.*

149. C MAJOR SCALE

155. MONDAY'S MELODY

Traditional Folk Song

Moderato

III I III I III

Fine

D.C. al Fine

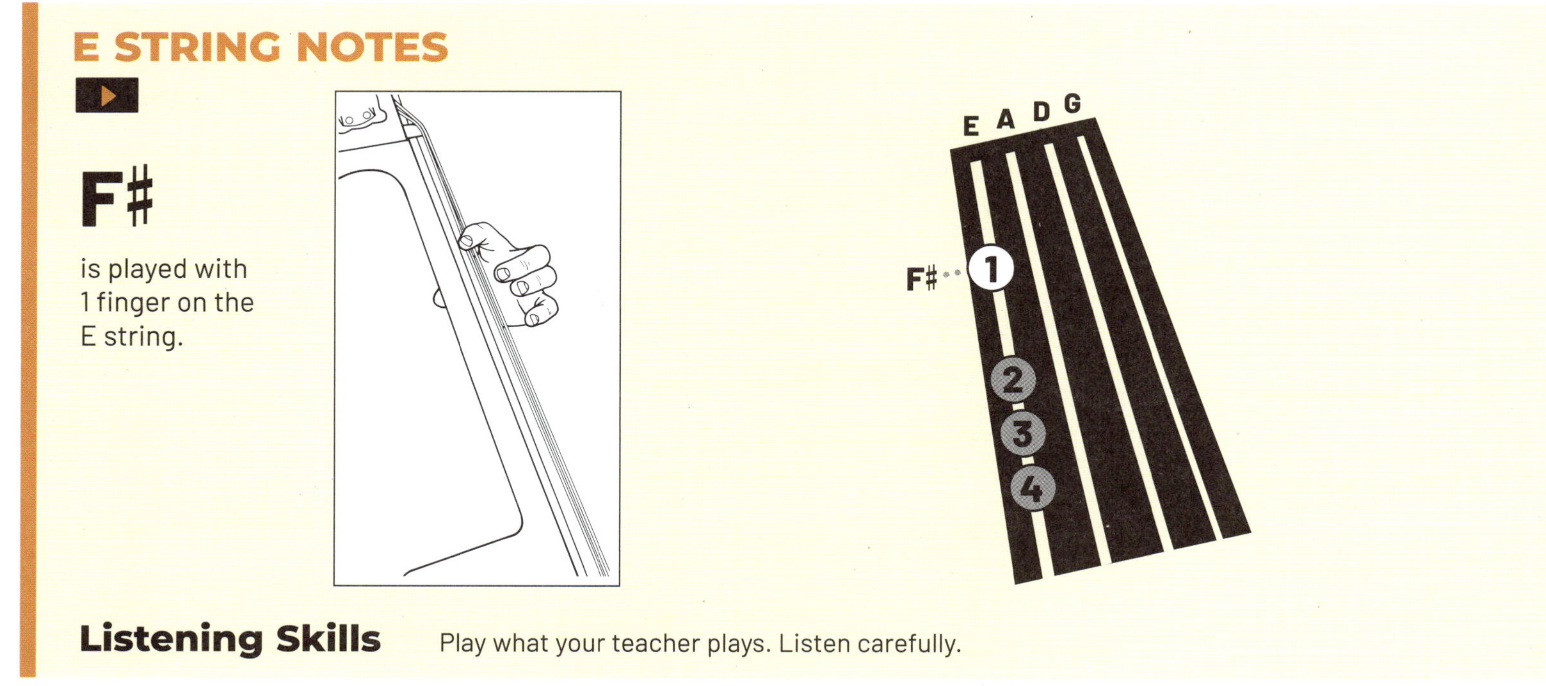

Listening Skills

Play what your teacher plays. Listen carefully.

156. LET'S READ "E"

157. LET'S READ "A" – Review

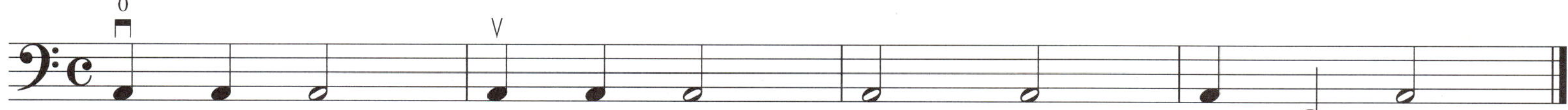

158. LET'S READ "G" – Review

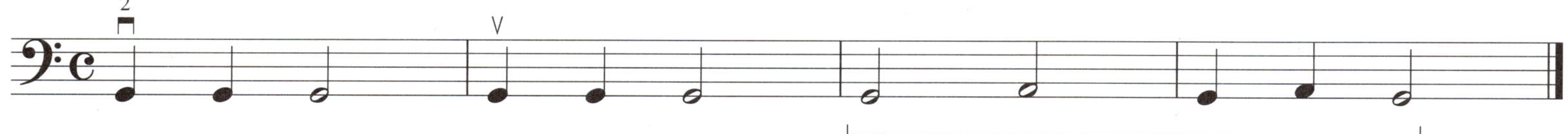

159. LET'S READ "F♯" (F-sharp)

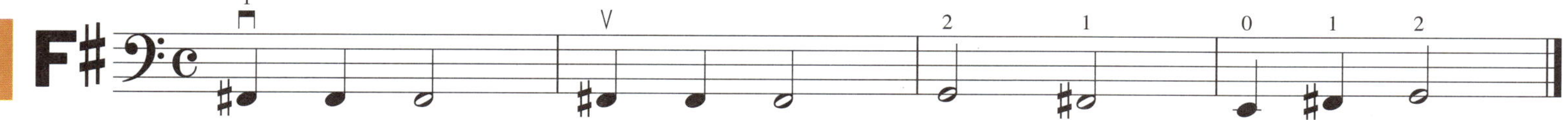

160. MOVING ALONG

Name the notes before you play.

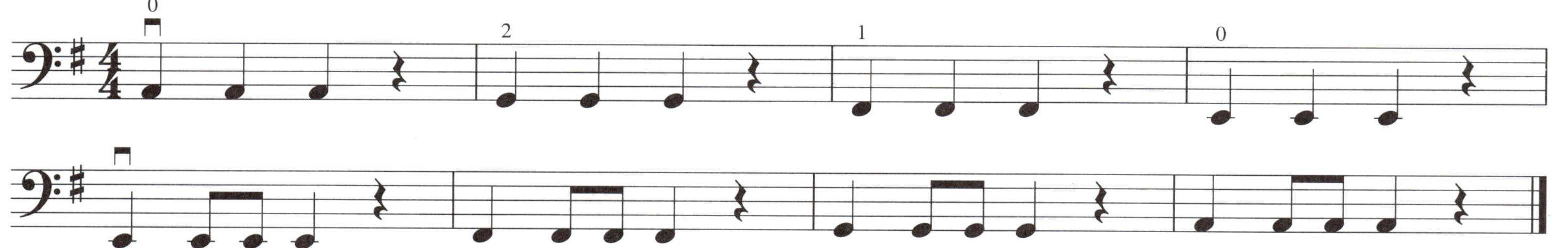

161. G MAJOR SCALE

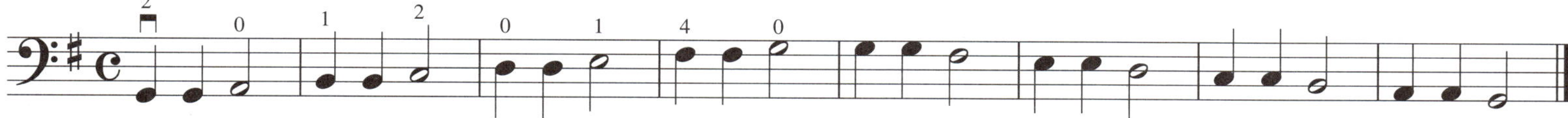

162. SHEPHERD'S HEY

English Folk Song

Moderato

163. BIG ROCK CANDY MOUNTAIN

American Folk Song

Allegro

Listening Skills Play what your teacher plays. Listen carefully.

164. LET'S READ "B" – Review

165. ICE SKATING

Moderato

166. ESSENTIAL ELEMENTS QUIZ – ACADEMIC FESTIVAL OVERTURE THEME

Johannes Brahms

Moderato

Additional bonus songs are available online. See the inside front cover for details.

Staccato

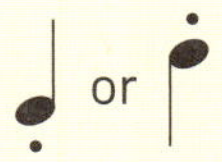

Staccato notes are marked with a dot above or below the note. A staccato note is played with a stopped bow stroke. Listen for a space between staccato notes.

167. PLAY STACCATO

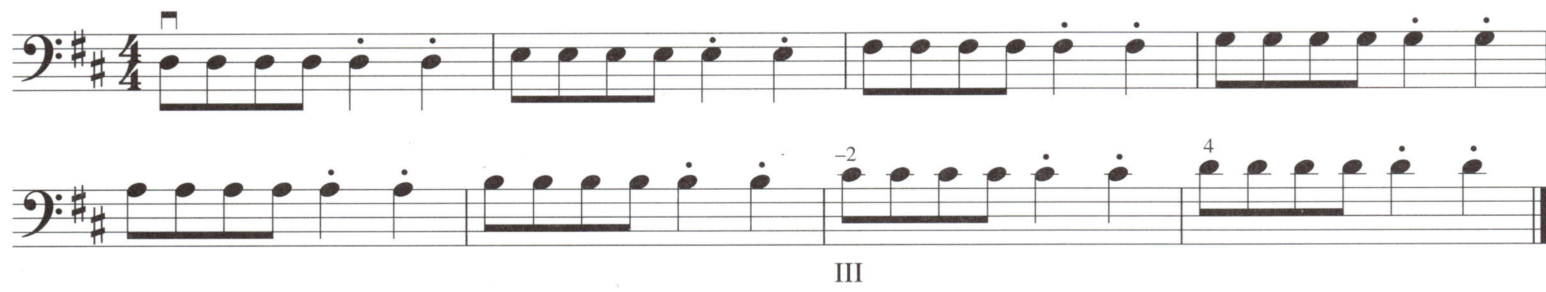

168. ARKANSAS TRAVELER

Southern American Folk Song

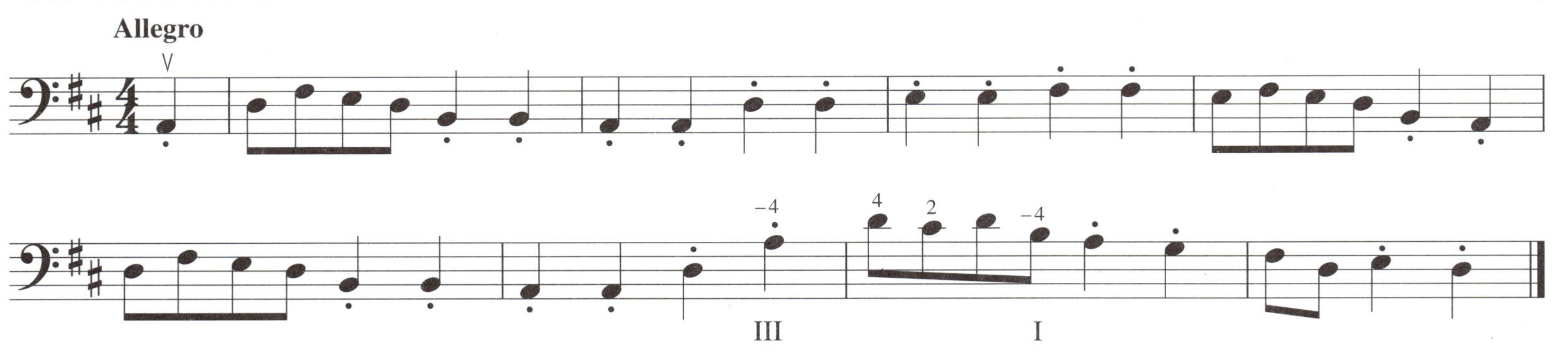

SKILL BUILDERS – G Major

169.

170.

171.

172.

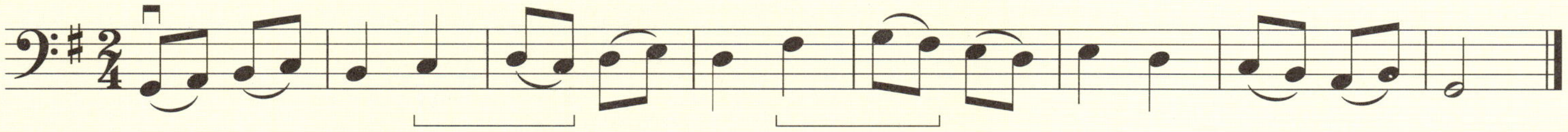

173.

Hooked Bowing

Hooked bowing is two or more notes played in the same direction with a stop between each note.

174. HOOKED ON D MAJOR

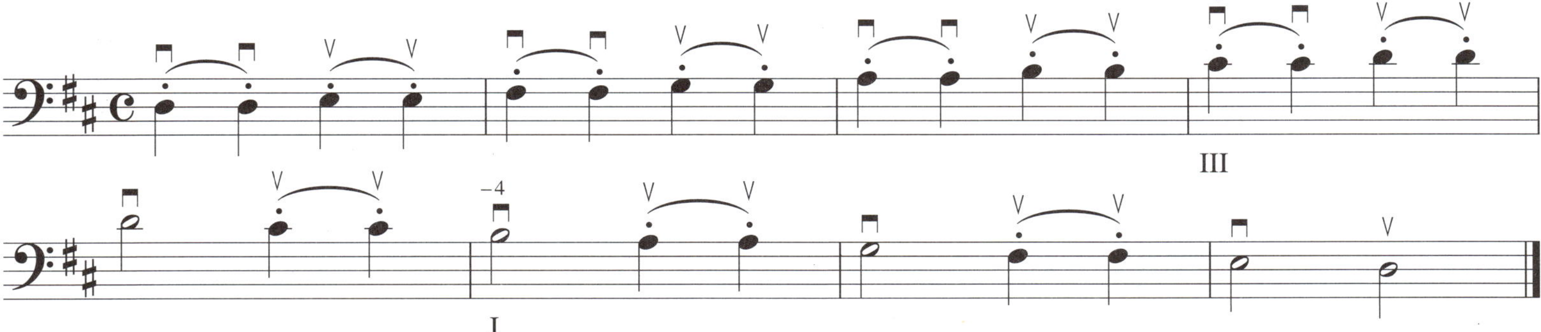

175. WALTZING BOWS

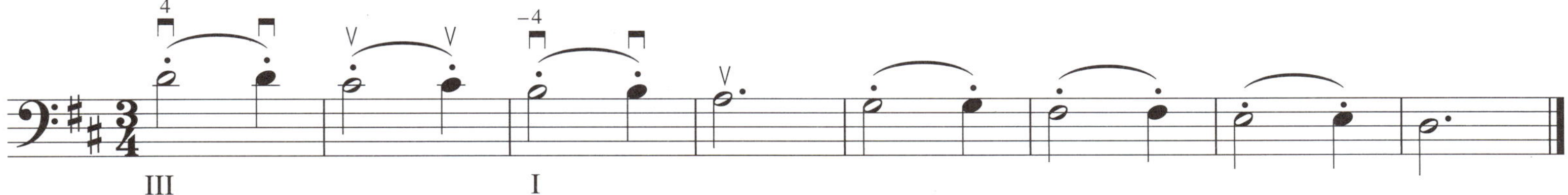

176. POP GOES THE WEASEL

American Folk Song

Allegro

SKILL BUILDERS – C Major

177.

II I

178.

II I

179.

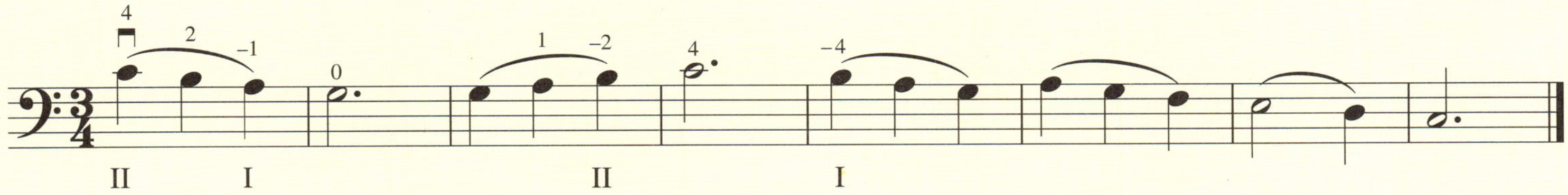

II I II I

180.

II I II

Dynamics

Dynamics tell us what volume to play or sing.

f (*forte*) Play loudly. Add more weight to the bow.

p (*piano*) Play softly. Remove weight from the bow.

181. FORTE AND PIANO

182. SURPRISE SYMPHONY THEME

Franz Josef Haydn

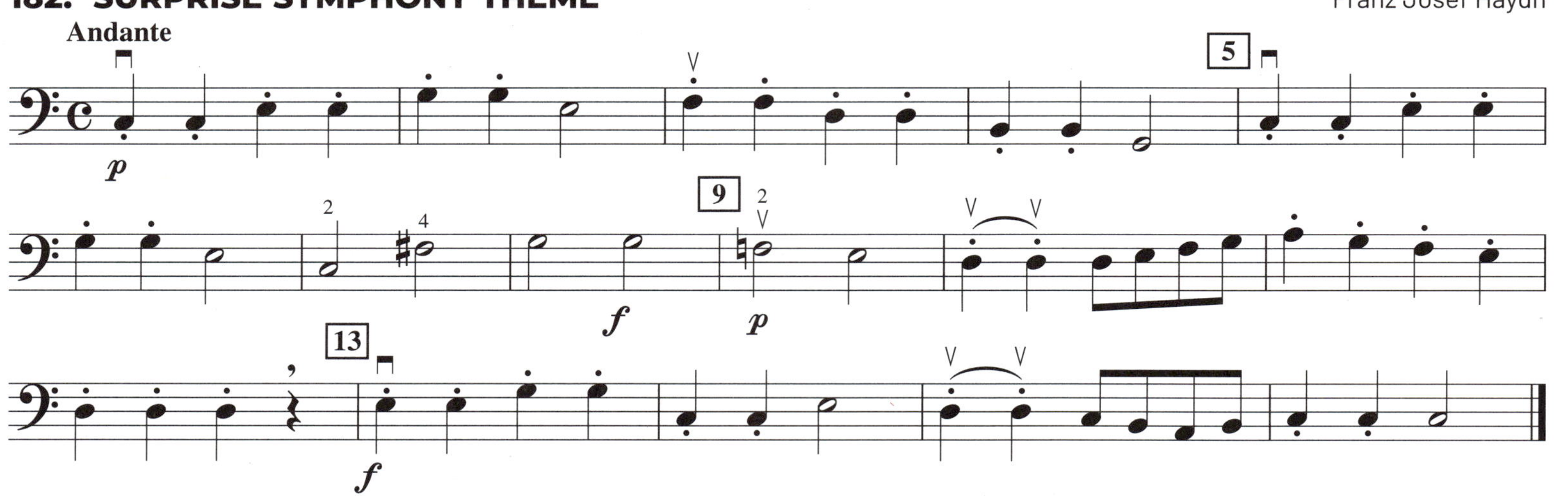

SKILL BUILDERS – Scales and Arpeggios

Add your own dynamics to any of the lines below.

183. D MAJOR

184. G MAJOR

185. G MAJOR *(Upper Octave - violin)*

186. C MAJOR

187. C MAJOR *(Lower Octave - viola and cello)*

PERFORMANCE SPOTLIGHT

188. CRIPPLE CREEK – Orchestra Arrangement (A = Melody and B = Harmony)

American Folk Song
Arr. Michael Allen

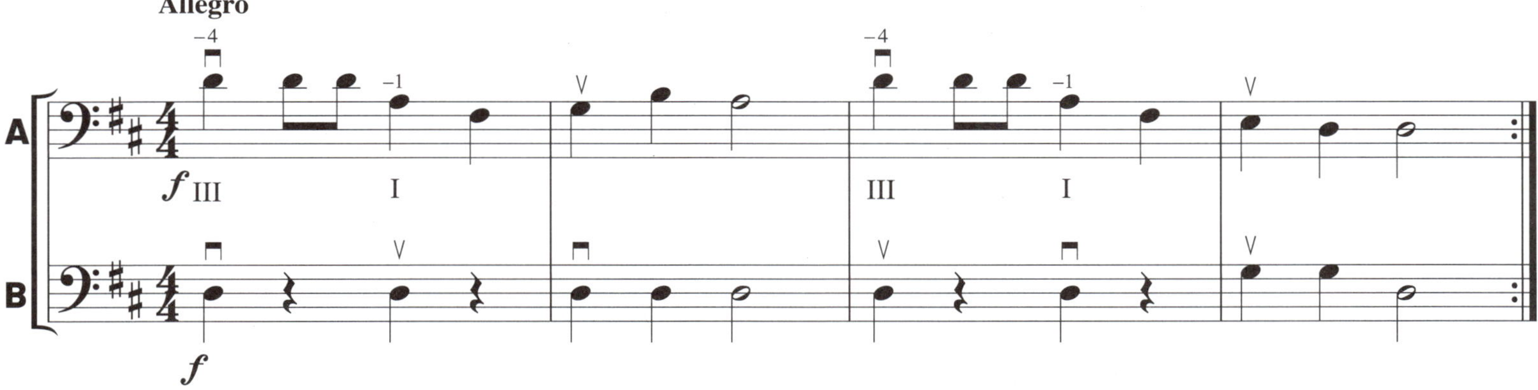

Africa is a large continent made up of many nations, and African folk music is as diverse as its many cultures. This folk song is from Kenya. The words describe warriors as they prepare for battle. Listen to examples of African folk music and describe the sound.

HISTORY

189. TEKELE LOMERIA – Orchestra Arrangement

Kenyan Warrior Song
Arr. John Higgins

PERFORMANCE SPOTLIGHT

HISTORY

Italian composer **Gioachino Rossini** (1792–1868) wrote some of the world's favorite operas. "William Tell" was Rossini's last opera, and its popular theme is still heard on television.

190. WILLIAM TELL OVERTURE – Orchestra Arrangement

Gioachino Rossini
Arr. John Higgins

Allegro

A

B

Fine

9

D.C. al Fine

191. ROCKIN' STRINGS – Orchestra Arrangement

John Higgins

Moderato

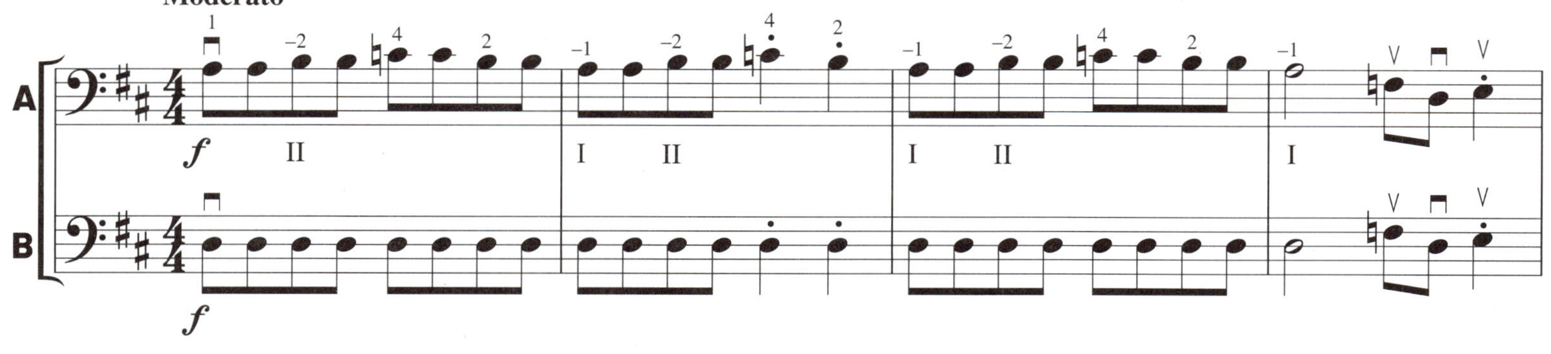

PERFORMANCE SPOTLIGHT

192. SIMPLE GIFTS – Orchestra Arrangement

Shaker Folk Song
Arr. John Higgins

Andante

A
B

f
f

4
-4
f III
I

10
p

f
f

19
-4
2
-4
III
I
p
p

PERFORMANCE SPOTLIGHT

Solo with Piano Accompaniment

A solo is a composition written for one player, often with piano accompaniment. This solo was written by **Johann Sebastian Bach** (1685-1750). You and a piano accompanist can perform for the orchestra, your school, your family and other occasions. When you have learned the piece well, try memorizing it. Performing for an audience is an excellent part of being involved in music.

Improvisation

Improvisation is the art of freely creating your own music as you play.

194. RHYTHM JAM *Using the following notes, improvise your own rhythms.*

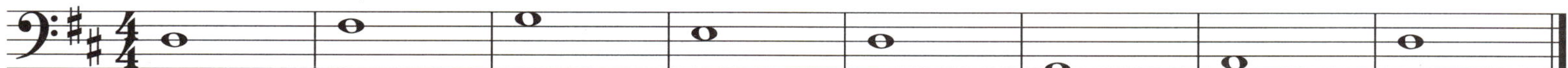

195. INSTANT MELODY *Using the following notes, improvise your own melody (Line A), to go with the accompaniment (Line B).*

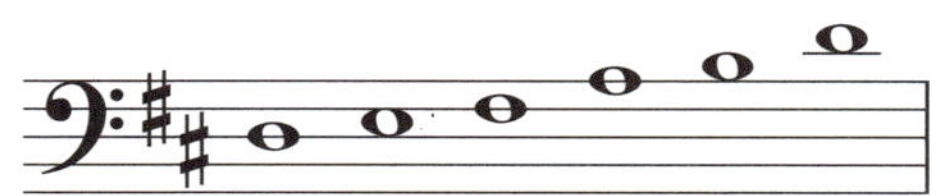

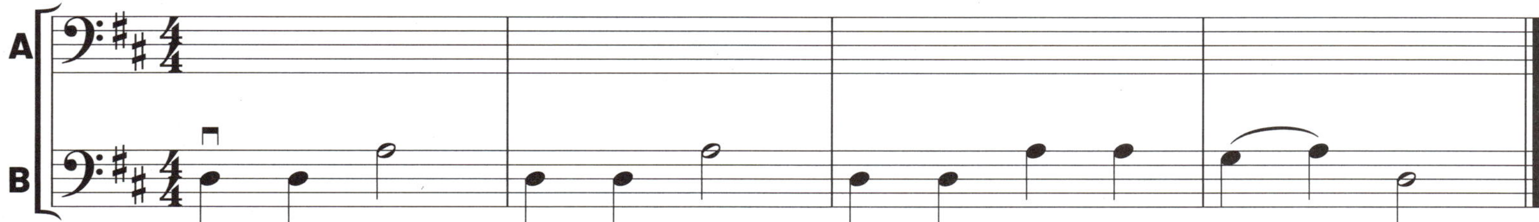

DOUBLE BASS FINGERING CHART

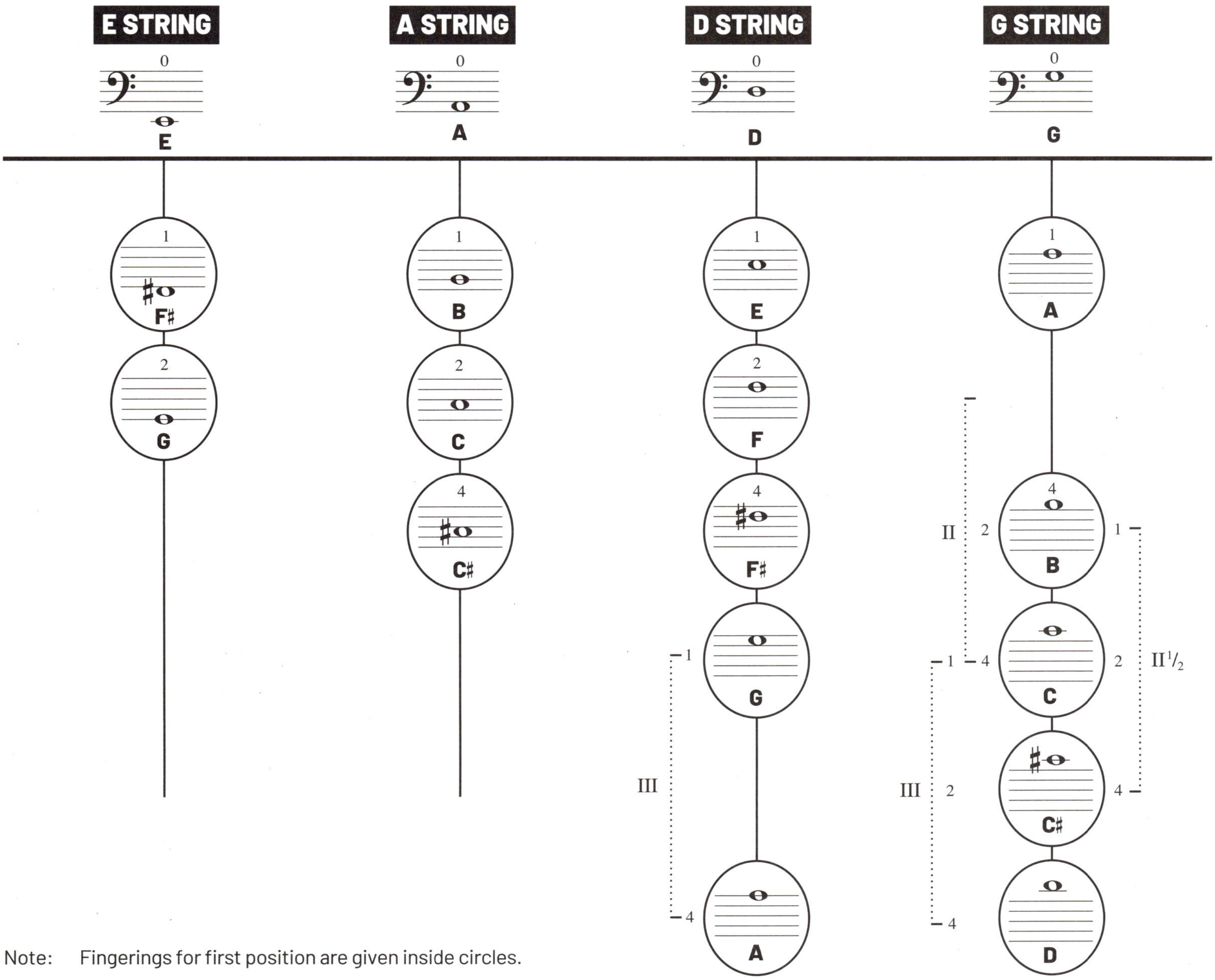

E STRING
- 0 — E
- 1 — F♯
- 2 — G

A STRING
- 0 — A
- 1 — B
- 2 — C
- 4 — C♯

D STRING
- 0 — D
- 1 — E
- 2 — F
- 4 — F♯
- G (III: 1)
- A (III: 4)

G STRING
- 0 — G
- 1 — A
- 4 — B (II: 2; II½: 1)
- C (II: 4; III: 1; II½: 2)
- C♯ (III: 2; II½: 4)
- D (III: 4)

Note: Fingerings for first position are given inside circles.

Reference Index

Definitions (pg.)

Composers

World Music